The Handy 5

Planning and Assessing Integrated Information Skills Instruction, Second Edition

Shelia K. Blume
Carol Fox
Jacqueline McMahon Lakin
Betsy Losey
Janis K. Stover

Edited by Betsy Losey

The Scarecrow Press, Inc.
Lanham, Maryland • Toronto • Plymouth, UK
2007

SCARECROW PRESS, INC.

Published in the United States of America by Scarecrow Press, Inc.
A wholly owned subsidiary of The Rowman & Littlefield Publishing Group, Inc.
4501 Forbes Boulevard, Suite 200, Lanham, Maryland 20706
www.scarecrowpress.com

Estover Road
Plymouth PL6 7PY
United Kingdom

British Library Cataloguing in Publication Information Available

Library of Congress Cataloging-in-Publication Data
The Handy 5 : planning and assessing integrated information skills instruction. — 2nd ed. / Shelia K. Blume ... [et al.] ; edited by Betsy Losey.
    p. cm.
  Rev. ed. of: The Handy 5 : planning and assessing integrated information skills instruction / Kansas Association of School Librarians. Research Committee.
  Includes bibliographical references and index.
  ISBN-13: 978-0-8108-5908-1 (pbk. : alk. paper)
  ISBN-10: 0-8108-5908-4 (pbk. : alk. paper)
 1. Information retrieval–Study and teaching–United States. 2. Information literacy–Study and teaching–United States. 3. Information literacy–Standards–United States.
4. School libraries–Activity programs–United States–Evaluation. 5. School librarian participation in curriculum planning–United States. 6. Instructional materials personnel–United States–Handbooks, manuals, etc. I. Blume, Shelia K. II. Losey, Betsy.
III. Kansas Association of School Librarians. Research Committee. Handy 5.
IV. Title: Handy Five.
ZA3075.K36 2007
025.5'24'071–dc22   2007002183

⊖™The paper used in this publication meets the minimum requirements of American National Standard for Information Sciences—Permanence of Paper for Printed Library Materials, ANSI/NISO Z39.48-1992.
Manufactured in the United States of America.

Contents

Preface

The Handy 5 was born of a need that began in 1991, when the Kansas State Board of Education initiated a statewide school improvement process, the Quality Performance Accreditation system. Unlike past accreditation methods, which focused on such things as the number of books in libraries or the square footage of buildings, Kansas accredits schools based on student performance; i.e., a school's quality is judged by its students' academic performance and their continual academic improvement. Furthermore, the Quality Performance Accreditation system requires all educators to collaborate in the design, implementation, and assessment of instruction. For school library media specialists, the new challenge was to evaluate performance by measuring student learning of information skills. However, no system or model existed for the systematic measuring of these skills, which were now the province of school library media specialists.

When the Kansas Association of School Librarians (KASL) formed a research committee in 1994 to conduct necessary research for library media specialists in the state, informal interviews with leading library media specialists indicated a need for a model to plan and assess the teaching of information skills. This need became the focus for the KASL Research Committee.

HOW THE MODEL WAS CREATED

From 1994 to 1995, the KASL Research Committee conducted a literature review and found no interdisciplinary model for assessing learning. However, the search did reveal a number of articles and books that discussed performance assessment, and these titles contributed to the group's general understanding of assessment and served as a foundation for the development of a preliminary assessment model.

During the summer of 1995, the committee organized a two-day summer institute to define an interdisciplinary model for assessing learning across the curriculum. An invitation was issued statewide to library media specialists interested in participating; they were in turn encouraged to invite interested teachers and administrators in their schools. Special invitations were extended to subject area consultants at the Kansas State Department of Education. When the institute convened, twenty-five teachers, administrators, and Kansas State Department of Education curriculum specialists shared information skills models and assessment literature. As a result of the institute, the Research Committee derived a rough draft of a model, which the committee refined at an all-day meeting in August 1995.

During the fall of 1995, the committee met to review and refine the model, including the rubrics for assessment. After revising the model, committee members presented the model for reactions at six regional workshops sponsored by KASL. Feedback from these presentations was favorable, and suggestions were incorporated in a second revision of the model in January 1996.

EVALUATION AND REVISION OF THE MODEL

During the spring of 1996, the committee received the AASL/Highsmith Research Award to test the model in a sample of Kansas schools. The research is summarized in chapter 8.

After the research was finalized and the model adopted, the Research Committee began implementation. Presentations on the model and its use were given at several AASL national conferences, Kansas Library Conferences, and school district inservices over the next few years. It was soon discovered that the model is not a static document; new ideas for implementation were suggested and better ways of collaboration were discovered. National educational initiatives were mandated which have a direct impact on school libraries and their place in the lives of students. Over the years since the model was first introduced, the use of the methodology based on the initial research continues to support the idea that students can learn a process that will make them lifelong learners, and the library media specialist needs to be involved in the collaborative and teaching process of the school.

The KASL Research Committee became the Handy 5 Marketing Committee in order to continue the use and support of the model. It was at the impetus of this committee in 2006 that the new ideas and suggestions that resulted from use of the model be incorporated into a second edition.

USING THE HANDY 5

By using the Handy 5 integrated assessment model, library media specialists are involved in planning, implementing, and evaluating integrated information skills instruction. Traditionally, library media specialists may have designed the assignment, but their role is now more involved, with planning strategies for completing the assignment, using information resources, and helping the student complete the assignment. However, assessment has been left almost solely to the classroom teacher. Use of the Handy 5 encourages the library media specialist to be engaged in assessment in all stages of the learning/teaching process.

PURPOSE OF THE BOOK

Information skills instruction is a fundamental and vital part of K-12 education in the twenty-first century. As information specialists, library media specialists have a leadership role in teaching these skills. The Handy 5 has been demonstrated to be an effective model for planning, teaching, and assessing information skills instruction. Successful implementation of the Handy 5 integrated assessment model requires library media specialists and teachers to reconsider their roles in working with students. If we truly believe that all students can learn and that the role of teachers and library media specialists is to enhance learning, new ways of structuring the learning process must include systematic and frequent assessment throughout the learning process. Our five-step model provides a framework for planning learning activities to accommodate frequent and systematic evaluation for the benefit of the students' success. The purpose of part one of this book is to explain the Handy 5. Part two outlines the theoretical background and presents research that evaluated the model. Finally, part three provides useful examples of the model's implementation.

Shelia K. Blume
Carol Fox
Jacqueline McMahon Lakin
Betsy Losey
Janis K. Stover

Acknowledgments

The first edition of this book, and the research that enabled its writing, is the result of collaboration by the Kansas Association of School Librarians (KASL) Research Committee, KASL officers and members, and the numerous library media specialists, teachers, and students who enthusiastically worked with us on the project.

The Handy 5 Marketing Committee members, who also serve as writers and editors of the second edition, are still indebted to the Kansas Association of School Librarians for its endorsement of the project.

Committee members also appreciate the work done by the KASL District Directors and Directors-Elect for their help in marketing *The Handy 5* at the fall workshops. We thank those school districts that invited committee members to present inservice sessions and who then adopted the Handy 5 as the problem-solving model for their schools. The addition of new lesson plan examples would not be possible without the help of students enrolled in library science classes at Emporia State University and Fort Hays State University.

PILOT SCHOOLS AND LIBRARY MEDIA SPECIALISTS

Credit is still given to the ten schools and their library media specialists who enthusiastically became a part of the pilot project by implementing it in their schools. Their principals supported them in their work. The following professionals were the "stars" of our project:

Pat Booth, *Jay Shideler Elementary School, Washburn Rural School District, KS*
Sherry Deaton, *Wathena High School, Wathena, KS*
Jane Dickerson, *Morse Elementary School, Blue Valley, KS*
Carolyn Hansen, *Wathena Elementary School, Wathena, KS*
Kathy Hodgson, *Little River School, Little River, KS*
Denise Irwin, *Andover High School, Andover, KS*
Juanita Jameson, *Holcomb Elementary School, Holcomb, KS*
Latane C. Kreiser, *Fort Riley Middle School, Fort Riley, KS*
Debbi Maddy, *Bonner Springs High School, Bonner Springs, KS*
Judy Wilbert, *Anderson Elementary School, Wichita, KS*

UNIT PLANS

Many library media specialists and students continue to respond to our request for lesson plans using *The Handy 5* and *The Handy 3*. We are grateful to the students in Shelia Blume's school library media classes at Fort Hays State University and to the students in Carol Fox's school library media class at Emporia State University. In addition, we thank the following library media specialists who contributed their creative application of *The Handy 5*.

In chapter 6, Betsy Losey, a retired elementary school librarian, created the "Treasures of the Sea" unit. In chapter 3, Denise Irwin, Andover High School, Andover, Kansas, created the English unit. Jan Prather, Washington Elementary School, El Dorado, Kansas, submitted the third-grade unit.

EDITORIAL ASSISTANCE

Primarily the writing committee edited the second edition. Dr. Bob Grover, the KASL Research Committee Chair and lead researcher for the first edition, graciously agreed to read the new edition for continuity. Another lifetime supply of chocolates is due Shelia Blume, Carol Fox, Jackie Lakin, Betsy Losey, and Jan Stover who volunteered their time and expertise to update the original work.

PART ONE

The Model and
How to Use It

1

Overview of the Book

Need for the Model

Collaboratively Teaching Information Literacy

Purpose of the Book

Organization of the Book

NEED FOR THE MODEL

This book and the model that it focuses on grew out of a national need. During the 1980s, a nationwide movement toward outcomes based (sometimes called competency based or results based) education swept the country. We saw a renewed interest in assessment as part of that movement. Concurrently, the role of the library media specialist (LMS) was evolving from one of supporting the curriculum by providing instructional materials to integrating information skills instruction into subject area instruction. This role was reflected both In *Information Power* (1988) and in *Information Power: Building Partnerships for Learning* (1998). These latest national standards for school library media programs articulate the LMS's roles as teacher, instructional partner, information specialist, and program administrator. *Information Power: Building Partnerships for Learning* describes the teaching role as follows:

> The library media specialist is knowledgeable about current research on teaching and learning and skilled in applying its findings to a variety of situations–particularly those that call upon students to access, evaluate, and use information from multiple sources in order to learn, to think, and to create and apply new knowledge. (p. 4)

Parallel to the national trends for library media specialists (LMSs) to become engaged in the teaching of information skills integrated into subject areas at all grade levels, the Kansas Association of School Librarians (KASL) Research Committee, in collaboration with the Kansas State Department of Education, embarked on a project to develop a model for planning and assessing learning across the curriculum. The LMSs (generalists) are uniting with teachers (subject area or grade level specialists) to collaborate and to integrate the teaching of information skills into mathematics, social studies, science, language arts, and the arts. A tool is needed for LMSs to help them work with teachers in various subject areas to plan instructional units. Likewise, there is a need for a team of collaborators to evaluate the learning that results from their collaborative efforts; in other words, is the integration of information skills instruction into the subject areas effective?

COLLABORATIVELY TEACHING INFORMATION LITERACY

What are the information skills that can be taught collaboratively with classroom teachers? According to *Information Power: Building Partnerships for Learning* (p. 1), information literacy is "the ability to find and use information–the keystone for lifelong learning." Numerous models exist for defining information literacy; e.g., the Big Six (Eisenberg and Berkowitz 1990) and Kuhlthau's Information Search Process model (Kuhlthau 1994). Although these models define steps in the effective use of information, they do not effectively address the need to plan and assess instruction of information literacy skills. However, the established role of the LMS as instructional partner requires the LMS to make linkages between the learning outcomes in the various subject areas and the learning of information skills. More specifically, the new national standards articulate the teaching and assessing role of the LMS as follows:

> Committed to the process of collaboration, the library media specialist works closely with individual teachers in the critical areas of designing authentic learning tasks and assessments and integrating the information and communication abilities required to meet subject matter standards. (*Information Power: Building Partnerships for Learning*, p. 5)

The question "How can LMSs and teachers collaboratively plan and assess learning?" guided the Research Committee as we reviewed the literature of education and library information studies. Although a great deal of education literature is devoted to assessment, little has been written on the assessment of information skills or on collaborative planning of instructional units. No comprehensive model for interdisciplinary assessment was found.

Consequently, the Research Committee set out to invent its own model, resulting in the creation of the Handy 5.

PURPOSE OF THE BOOK

This book was written to help LMSs and teachers to collaborate more effectively in the teaching of information skills. The need that prompted development of the Handy 5–a tool to provide a common language and assessment guidelines for integrating the teaching of information skills– is the same need that prompted writing this book. It is intended to be a readily understandable guide to the model's use by LMSs and teachers working with students to teach information skills. In addition to a clear explanation of the model, the book provides numerous examples of units that have been used successfully and are adaptable for use in your school.

ORGANIZATION OF THE BOOK

This book is written by practicing LMSs who have used the Handy 5, and they share unit plans and planning forms that have worked for them. The book is divided into three parts in a way that should help you, the reader, to use it effectively.

Part One: The Model and How to Use It

- Overview of the Book
- Introduction of the Handy 5 Model
- The Handy 5 in Kid Talk

- Using the Model at the Primary Level: The Handy 3
- Applying the Handy 5 in the Classroom
- The Model as a Collaborative Planning Tool

Part Two: Why the Model Is Important

- Trends in Education Today
- Using the Model: What Our Research Told Us

Part Three: The Model in Action

- Sample Lesson Plans

Since this book is written by and for LMSs and teachers, this introduction is as brief as possible so that you can get on to the important stuff–the model itself and how you can use it.

REFERENCES

American Association of School Librarians and Association for Educational Communications and Technology. *Information Power.* Chicago: American Library Association, 1988.

———. *Information Power: Building Partnerships for Learning.* Chicago: American Library Association, 1998.

Eisenberg, Michael B., and Robert E. Berkowitz. *Information Problem Solving: The Big Six Skills Approach to Library and Information Skills Instruction.* Norwood, NJ: Ablex, 1990.

Kuhlthau, Carol C. *Assessment and the School Library Media Center.* Englewood, CO: Libraries Unlimited, 1994.

———. *Seeking Meaning: A Process Approach to Library and Information Services.* Norwood, NJ: Ablex, 1994.

2

Introduction of the Handy 5 Model

The Problem

In Search of Common Language

Steps of the Handy 5 Defined

Designing Rubrics for an Integrated Assessment Model

The Handy 5 Model

Summary

THE PROBLEM

Information Power: Building Partnerships for Learning (1998) emphasizes the teaching of information skills integrated into subject area instruction. A common language, or model, is needed to enable grade level or curricular area teachers and LMSs to communicate effectively as they plan units of instruction. A common language is also needed for students to understand the problem-solving process that evolves during learning.

To develop a model to plan and assess learning across the curriculum, the Kansas Association of School Librarians (KASL) Research Committee, in collaboration with the Kansas State Department of Education, embarked on a research project in 1994. This committee conducted a literature review and developed a preliminary assessment model; in summer of 1995, the Committee organized a two-day institute to refine the model and to develop rubrics for an interdisciplinary model for assessing learning. During the following school year, the committee presented the model to numerous meetings of library media professionals and teachers to further refine the model. In the spring of 1996, the committee received the American Association of School Librarians/Highsmith Research Award to test the model in a sample of Kansas schools during the 1996-97 school year. This chapter describes an integrated teaching/learning model that has evolved from research and field-testing over a four-year period. Because of its components and ease of use, it has come to be called the Handy 5.

IN SEARCH OF A COMMON LANGUAGE

LMSs currently integrate knowledge of the learning outcomes of each discipline or level of education with outcomes for critical thinking and information problem-solving skills. Integration of instruction and assessment demands an understanding of the vocabulary of each discipline as well. The KASL Research Committee sought to find a common language among these subject areas: reading and writing, mathematics, social studies, science, the arts, and information literacy skills. In doing so, the Eisenberg/Berkowitz Big Six Problem-Solving Model was used as a basis for comparison. The Big Six presents six steps for problem solving:

1. Task Definition: Define the problem and identify the information requirements of the problem.

2. Information-Seeking Strategies: Determine the range of possible sources and evaluate the different possible sources to determine priorities.

3. Location and Access: Locate sources (intellectually and physically) and find information within sources.

4. Information Use: Engage (e.g., read, hear, view) the information in a source and extract information from a source.

5. Synthesis: Organize information from multiple sources and present the information.

6. Evaluation: Judge the product (effectiveness) and judge the information problem-solving process (efficiency) (Eisenberg and Berkowitz 1990, p. 24).

Using the Big Six as a springboard, the common language for interdisciplinary collaboration evolved from an examination of the teaching process and perusal of Kansas's state standards for reading and writing, mathematics, social studies, science, and the arts. The state standards in turn reflect national subject area standards. The Research Committee created the following model, which serves as the "common language" for these areas, with teaching as its focus. The teaching/learning model in figure 2-1 collapses the Big Six into the following five steps of the Handy 5:

Figure 2-1 The Big Six Influenced the Creation of the Handy 5

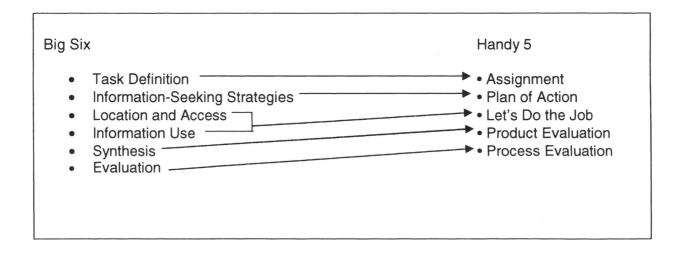

STEPS OF THE HANDY 5 DEFINED

All teacher/LMS collaborative teams begin with an **ASSIGNMENT.** This assignment aligns district and school curricular learning outcomes with appropriate discipline/grade level/unit outcomes. For planning instruction, this integrated assignment and its outcomes are directly tied to the completed product evaluation. For learning, a student must have a clear, complete understanding of the assignment or problem, which serves as a foundation for the plan of action, doing the job, and a successfully completed product.

The **PLAN OF ACTION** occurs when the teachers and the LMS determine which discipline-related, problem-solving, and instructional strategies are reasonable for the students to use in order to complete the assignment successfully. This step is also where the teacher and the LMS can assess what new information may be needed. The plan of action requires the students to choose the most appropriate strategy or strategies, and give reasons for this selection. The plan of action requires the students to analyze the various resources (printed, electronic, and human) that would enable them to successfully complete the assignment.

DOING THE JOB is implementation of the plan of action and combines step 3 (location and access) and step 4 (information use) of the Big Six. **DOING THE JOB** requires the teachers and the LMS to help the students focus on the assignment (the job) with all components in evidence. To do the job successfully, the students must demonstrate a clear understanding of the assignment/problem and apply the most appropriate strategy or strategies for completing the assignment.

The **PRODUCT EVALUATION,** determined by the LMS in collaboration with the teachers, is an assessment of the completed assignment. The product evaluation reflects the students' understanding of the assignment and application of the plan of action. This product (the completed assignment) may be a correct response to a question; the solution to a mathematical equation; a written, oral, or recorded report; a chart; a musical score; a cooperative learning project; a dance performance; a research paper; or an invention, as well as other formats. Typically a grade, score, or other rating is assigned, and the product evaluation is complete.

The **PROCESS EVALUATION,** which is conducted by the teachers and the LMS with the students' active participation, assesses the alignment of the assignment, the plan of action, doing the job, and the finished product. In other words, the teachers, the LMS, and students ask: *Does the student demonstrate an understanding of the assignment through a reasonable plan of action, which is appropriately applied in doing the job, and evident in the finished product?* Such assessment should provide opportunities for students to reflect on how to improve the quality of future assignments and, ultimately, real-life application.

The terms in the integrated teaching/learning model represent a common language for discussing and planning instruction with teachers from various subject areas. Based on the steps of the model, terms were organized and adapted from Kansas subject area standards to prepare the following table of comparisons (2-1).

Table 2-1 The Handy 5 Steps Applied Areas of Curriculum

Handy 5 Steps	Reading	Writing	Mathematics	Social Studies	Science	The Arts	Information Literacy Skills
Assignment	Read selection, read question	Develop ideas and content for audience	Understand the problem	Identify issue for investigation	Recognize and define the problem	Understand the problem	Define task
Plan of action	Outline key terms and concepts	Further develop ideas and content for audience	Choose problem—solving strategy	Develop a plan for the investigation	Design a problem-solving strategy	Design a plan to solve the problem	Develop information-seeking strategies
Doing the job	Choose appropriate information sources	Refine the voice including strategy flow; proofread	Implement a problem-solving strategy	Acquire information from sources; organize information	Implement a problem-solving strategy	Try out the plan	Locate, access, and use information
Product evaluation	Apply appropriate information source	Submit to editor, revise	Find and report conclusion	Choose and justify the issue; present results	Interpret and communicate findings and conclusions	Present the solution or product for evaluation	Synthesize and present the information
Process evaluation	Check response for understanding, accuracy, and completeness	Publish; evaluate for audience reception and logic	Evaluate conclusion for reasonableness of results	Evaluate process and product of the investigation	Evaluate findings for clarity, accuracy, and real-life applications	Evaluate the effectiveness of the process as it relates to the solution or product	Evaluate product (effectiveness) and process (efficiency)

DESIGNING RUBRICS FOR AN INTEGRATED ASSESSMENT MODEL

Numerous assessment strategies were reviewed by the Research Committee, resulting in the selection of rubrics for application in the integrated assessment model. Rubrics are guidelines for evaluation; they are intended to provide qualitative descriptions or measures of the student's progress toward stated outcomes. Rubrics were developed, submitted to practitioners for reaction, and revised. The Handy 5 uses a rubric based on four levels, plus a level of "not applicable/nothing available." A general description of the rubric, with level #4 as the highest level of achievement, follows:

Rating NA: There is no evidence that the student has attempted to do the work. There is no basis for evaluation.

Rating 1: The student demonstrates an awareness or knowledge of the process or product. There may be a misunderstanding or serious misconception, as indicated by evidence the teacher and the LMS have gathered.

Rating 2: The student demonstrates a partial or incomplete comprehension of the problem or process. Some components of the assignment are missing or incorrect.

Rating 3: Evidence provided by behavior and/or example(s) indicate that the student has a substantial and acceptable measure of learning. This is the benchmark, or expected level of achievement.

Rating 4: The student demonstrates a thorough and complete understanding; he has integrated the knowledge and is able to apply it in a real-life situation. This level of learning exceeds the benchmark, or expected level of achievement.

For each stage of the model, e.g., assignment, plan of action, the general rubric described above is adapted to each step. The rubrics for each stage of the model are presented in table 2-2. These rubrics, combined with the integrated teaching/learning model, provide LMSs and teachers with a tool for planning, implementing, and assessing the integrated teaching of information skills.

Table 2-2 Rubrics for the Handy 5

Assignment	Plan of Action	Doing the Job	Product Evaluation	Process Evaluation
4-Demonstrates thorough, complete understanding of assignment/problem	**4**-Chooses highly effective strategies to fulfill the assignment	**4**-Implements the plan of action in a highly effective manner	**4**-The product reflects the student's thorough, complete understanding of the problem	**4**-Evaluates the problem-solving process (steps 1-4) in a highly effective manner
3*-Demonstrates a substantial understanding of assignment/problem	**3***-Chooses effective strategies to fulfill the assignment	**3***-Implements the plan of action in an effective manner	**3***-The product reflects the student's substantial understanding of the problem	**3***-Evaluates the problem-solving process (steps 1-4) in an effective manner
2-Demonstrates a partial/incomplete understanding of assignment/problem	**2**-Chooses moderately effective strategies to fulfill the assignment	**2**-Implements the plan of action in a moderately effective manner	**2**-The product reflects the student's partial/incomplete understanding of the problem	**2**-Evaluates the problem-solving process (steps 1-4) in a moderately effective manner
1-Demonstrates a misunderstanding or serious misconception of the assignment/problem	**1**-Chooses ineffective strategy/ies to fulfill the assignment	**1**-Implements the plan of action in an ineffective manner	**1**-The product reflects the student's misunderstanding or serious misconception of the problem	**1**-Evaluates the problem-solving process (steps 1-4) in an ineffective manner
NA-Not applicable/nothing available	**NA**-Not applicable/nothing available	**NA**-Not applicable/nothing available	**NA**-Not applicable/nothing available	**NA**-Not applicable/nothing available

*Benchmark or mastery

THE HANDY 5 MODEL

Figure 2-2 is a five-part representation of each step of the Handy 5. Subject area terms from table 2-1 are integrated with rubric descriptions from table 2-2. These tables are helpful when presenting the Handy 5 to groups.

Figure 2-2 The Handy 5, Step One: Assignment

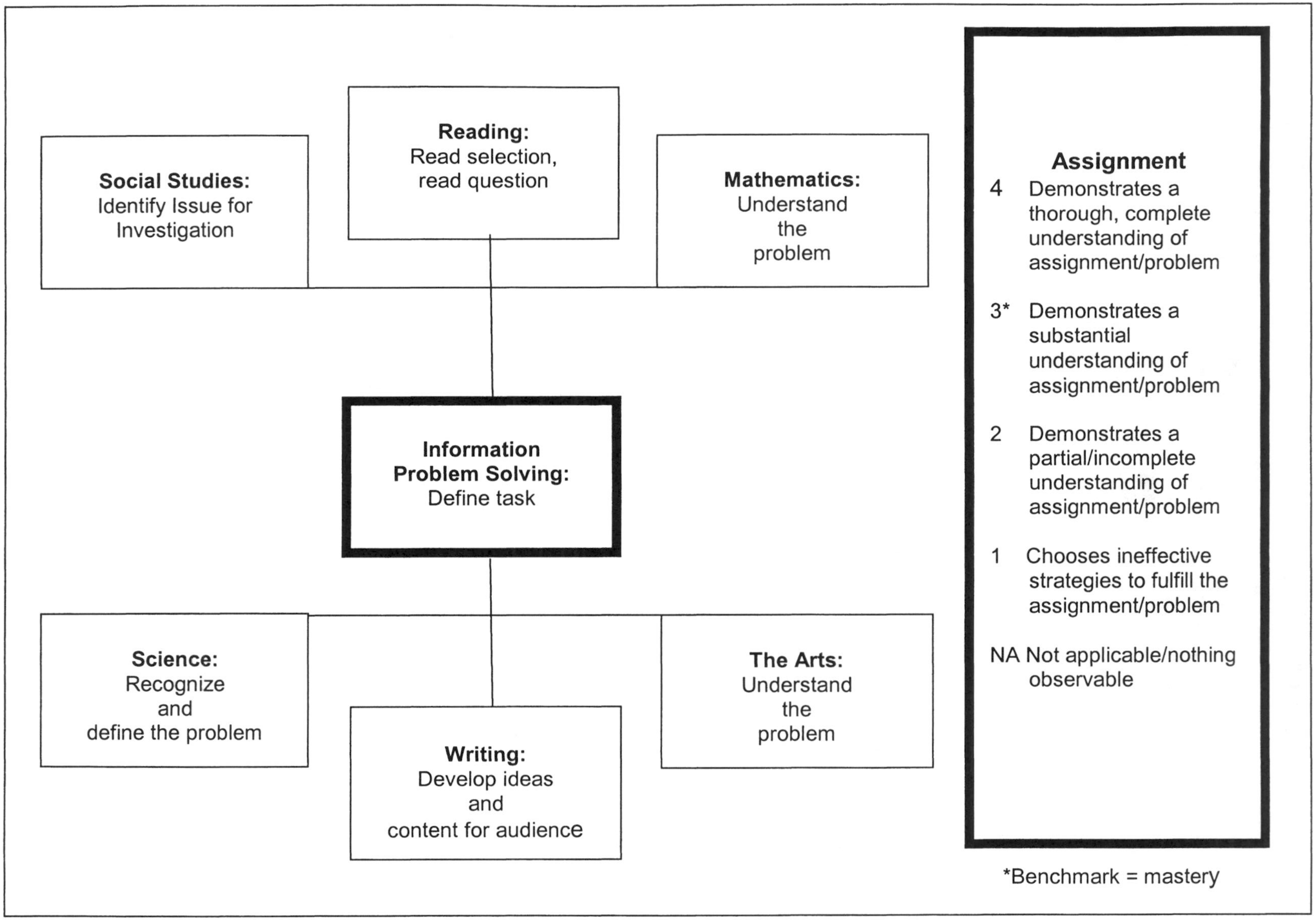

Social Studies:
Identify Issue for
Investigation

Reading:
Read selection,
read question

Mathematics:
Understand
the
problem

**Information
Problem Solving:**
Define task

Science:
Recognize
and
define the problem

Writing:
Develop ideas
and
content for audience

The Arts:
Understand
the
problem

Assignment

4   Demonstrates a
     thorough, complete
     understanding of
     assignment/problem

3*   Demonstrates a
     substantial
     understanding of
     assignment/problem

2   Demonstrates a
     partial/incomplete
     understanding of
     assignment/problem

1   Chooses ineffective
     strategies to fulfill the
     assignment/problem

NA   Not applicable/nothing
     observable

*Benchmark = mastery

Figure 2-2 (continued) The Handy 5, Step Two: Plan of Action

Social Studies:
Develop a
plan for
the investigation

Reading:
Outline key terms
and
concepts

Mathematics:
Choose a
problem-solving
strategy

**Information
Problem Solving:**
Develop information-
seeking strategies

Science:
Design a
problem-solving
strategy

Writing:
Further develop ideas
and content
for audience

The Arts:
Design a plan
to solve
the problem

Plan of Action

4 Chooses highly
   effective strategies to
   fulfill the assignment

3* Chooses effective
    strategies to fulfill the
    assignment

2 Chooses moderately
   effective strategies
   to fulfill the
   assignment

1 Chooses ineffective
   strategies to fulfill the
   assignment

NA Not applicable/nothing
   observable

*Benchmark = mastery

Figure 2-2 (continued) The Handy 5, Step Three: Let's Do the Job

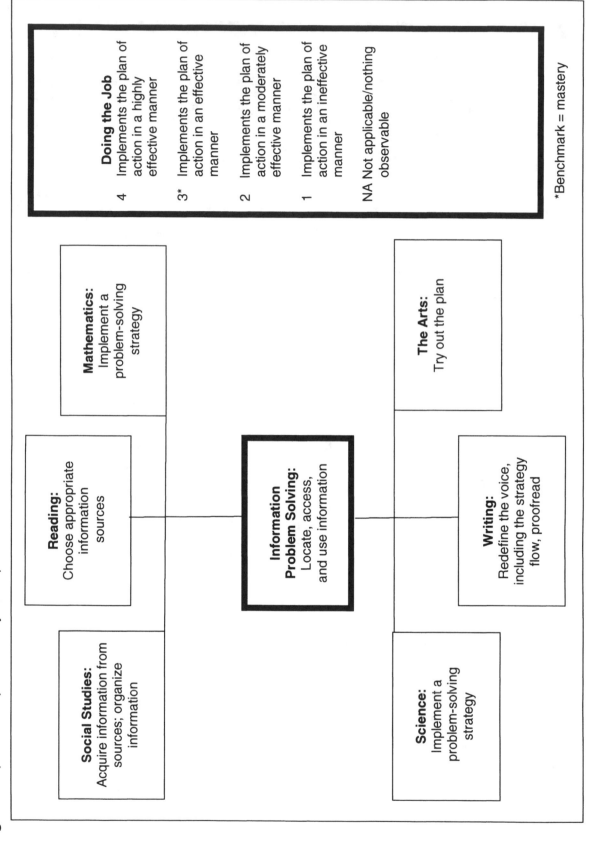

Doing the Job

4 Implements the plan of action in a highly effective manner

3* Implements the plan of action in an effective manner

2 Implements the plan of action in a moderately effective manner

1 Implements the plan of action in an ineffective manner

NA Not applicable/nothing observable

*Benchmark = mastery

Mathematics:
Implement a problem-solving strategy

The Arts:
Try out the plan

Reading:
Choose appropriate information sources

Information Problem Solving:
Locate, access, and use information

Writing:
Redefine the voice, including the strategy flow, proofread

Social Studies:
Acquire information from sources; organize information

Science:
Implement a problem-solving strategy

Figure 2-2 (continued) The Handy 5, Step Four: Product Evaluation

Product Evaluation

4   The product reflects the student's thorough, complete understanding of the problem

3* The product reflects the student's substantial understanding of the problem

2   The product reflects the student's partial/incomplete understanding of the problem

1   The product reflects the student's misunderstanding or serious misconception of the problem

NA Not applicable/nothing observable

*Benchmark = mastery

Mathematics: Find and report conclusions

The Arts: Present the solution or product for evaluation

Reading: Apply appropriate information sources

Information Problem Solving: Synthesize and present the information

Writing: Submit to editor, revise

Social Studies: Choose and justify the issue; present results

Science: Interpret and communicate findings and conclusions

Figure 2-2 (continued) The Handy 5, Step Five: Process Evaluation

Social Studies:
Evaluate process and production of the investigation

Reading:
Check response for understanding, accuracy, and completeness

Mathematics:
Evaluate conclusion for reasonableness of results

Information Problem Solving:
Evaluate process and product

Science:
Evaluate findings for clarity, accuracy, and real-life applications

Writing:
Publish; evaluate for audience reception and logic

The Arts:
Evaluate the effectiveness of the process as it relates to the solution or product

Process Evaluation

4 Evaluates the problem-solving process (steps 1-4) in a highly effective manner

3* Evaluates the problem-solving process (steps 1-4) in an effective manner

2 Evaluates the problem-solving process (steps 1-4) in a moderately effective manner

1 Evaluates the problem-solving process (steps 1-4) in an ineffective manner

NA Not applicable/nothing observable

*Benchmark = mastery

SUMMARY

Recognition of the need for a common language between LMSs and teachers led to the examination of available models and finally to the development of the Handy 5. By focusing on teaching and including an assessment component, this approach offers a valid, reliable, and practical vehicle that provides the common language that enables teachers and LMSs to plan and assess collaboratively. The model began as an effort to bring common understanding to the need for collaboration and has served to solidify the library media specialist's role in this collaboration process.

REFERENCES

American Association of School Librarians and Association for Educational Communications and Technology. *Information Power: Building Partnerships for Learning.* Chicago: American Library Association, 1998.

Eisenberg, Michael B. and Robert E. Berkowitz. *Information Problem Solving: The Big Six Skills Approach to Library and Information Skills Instruction.* Norwood, NJ: Ablex, 1990.

3

The Handy 5 in Kid Talk

The Handy 5 in Kid Talk

Step 1: What Am I Supposed to Do?

Step 2: How Do I Get the Job Done?

Step 3: Let's Do the Job!

Step 4: What Do I Have to Show for It?

Step 5: How Well Did I Do?

Summary

THE HANDY 5 IN KID TALK

As noted in the findings in part two, chapter 8, the Handy 5 has proven an effective problem-solving tool. It can be used with students of all ages but should be adapted for use with primary age children (chapter 4). The model speaks directly to Information Literacy Standards 1, 2, and 3 for Student Learning:

Standard 1: The student who is information literate accesses information efficiently and effectively.

Standard 2: The student who is information literate evaluates information critically and competently.

Standard 3: The student who is information literate uses information accurately and creatively (*Information Power: Building Partnerships for Learning* 1998, p. 8).

Chapter 6 details how to apply the model as a planning instrument. This chapter deals with a step-by-step plan that students at all levels can follow in retrieving information. As the model becomes internalized, students will find it is a helpful problem-solving tool that works not only on most classroom assignments but also in solving real-world, everyday problems. Such internalization works best when the model is consistently used and adopted school-wide.

Presentation of the complete model provides an overview of the process, which gives a framework for the student's understanding. Individual steps can be covered in depth as the assignment progresses. Some lessons may concentrate on certain steps of the model; other lessons may include the entire plan.

A real-world example is an excellent way to introduce the entire model. For presenting the model to adults who might be using the Handy 5, such examples as buying a car, planning a vacation, and remodeling a home have provided useful ways to bring about familiarity with the steps of the model.

For presenting the model to students, consider such real-world applications as choosing a college for high school seniors, choosing a video game system or a cell phone for middle school students, spending allowance on a toy or deciding what afternoon snacks are good for you for the elementary level students.

A literature application has also proved helpful. Think about the story of the three little pigs. What was their assignment? The students will usually respond that the job was to build a house. When step 2 is introduced, students will be led to see that no real plan of action was in place, with dire repercussions in the case of the first two houses when it came to step 3. This is a good place to emphasize the importance of a plan of action and to mention that the plan is fluid and may need to be refined or changed to fit the circumstances. Step 4 gives them a look at a solid product that finally withstands the wolf. Step 5 is open to interpretation by the students of how the action of the three little pigs might be different the next time!

Most storylines follow the Handy 5 loosely. A problem (assignment) is set forth; the characters develop some means for solving the problem (plan of action). The bulk of the story reflects their attempts to solve (doing the job), culminating with the climax (product) when the problem is solved, either successfully or unsuccessfully. Many stories are a little short on process evaluation, but generally speaking, there is always a wrap-up paragraph or two that may constitute a process evaluation. More information on adapting the model to the younger students will be found in chapter 4.

Figure 3-1 is a visual interpretation of the model that has worked well. The complete unit for Animal Habitats and Literary Criticism can be found in chapter 9. Additional resources for teaching the Handy 5 are located at the end of this chapter, figures 12-15. Everyone has a tool that they carry with him or her all the time: a hand. Each step of the original model has been translated into "kid talk" and fits the fingers of the hand: the Handy 5.

Figure 3-1 The Handy 5 in "Kid Talk"

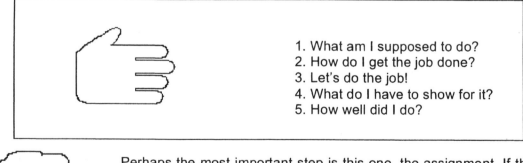

1. What am I supposed to do?
2. How do I get the job done?
3. Let's do the job!
4. What do I have to show for it?
5. How well did I do?

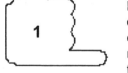

Perhaps the most important step is this one, the assignment. If the students don't understand the assignment, they will have very little hope of carrying it out successfully. In knowing what the assignment is, they must also know what the expectations are for the end product. Take time to clarify the step by asking questions such as:

- What are the parameters of the assignment?
- What is the time schedule?
- What new terms are there?
- What questions do I need to answer?
- What should the end product look like?

This is a good place for the teacher to assess what *prior knowledge* the student brings to the assignment and to make time for review if deemed necessary.

This step may be assessed informally by having the students orally repeat back the components of the assignment or by showing thumbs-up or down to signify understanding of the assignment. The teacher then may ask for clarification questions from those who indicated thumbs down.

Formal assessment may take the form of a written paragraph by the students of their understanding of the assignment's components. Another method is completing a graphic organizer that helps students determine an actual topic after considering relevant questions.

As a rule, primary students function more successfully in the informal assessment area. Intermediate and middle school students like the confidence that completing a graphic organizer seems to bring. Figure 3-2 gives third-grade students an overview of what is expected of them in an animal habitat unit; the teacher used the thumbs-up down to indicate understanding:

Figure 3-2 Presentation of an Assignment: Third-Grade—Animal Habitat Project

---

I Can Do It Myself Rap

What am I supposed to do?
A diorama, paragraph, and poem too.
How do I get the job done?
Make a timeline; it will be fun.
LET'S GET THE JOB DONE! LET'S GET THE JOB DONE!
What do I have to show for it?
An animal habitat project just for you
What did I learn? How well did I do?

At the high school level, a written paragraph is a quick method that gives the teacher documentation that may contribute to the overall evaluation. For example, when the model was piloted, one English student wrote in her paragraph that she really didn't understand the assignment at all. The teacher was able to meet with the student on an individual basis and clarify the questions she had. Without the feedback, the student might not have voiced her confusion and might have gone on to try to complete the assignment in a haphazard manner. Figure 3-3 is an example of such a paragraph.

Figure 3-3 Presentation of an Assignment: Tenth-Grade—Literary Criticism

---

Due October 30
Prior to beginning any task, it is important to fully understand what is expected of you. What are the parameters? What is the time schedule? What new terms are there? What questions do you need to answer? What should the end product look like?

Write a complete description of the Literary Criticism project. Exactly what are the requirements you need to meet?

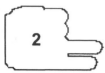

This is the plan of action. Some of the clarifying questions include:

- What resources will I need?
- Where should I look first?
- Which sources would be the most productive?
- How will I evaluate the applicability of the resources?
- Does my plan fit the assignment?

In this electronic age, finding information has become easier than ever. The focus for getting the job done has shifted from merely locating resources to evaluating the information these resources contain.

The success of this step depends on the presentation of available resources. The classroom teacher and LMS work collaboratively to present not only the possible resources, but also some method of evaluating their usefulness.

At the elementary and middle school levels, whole class decisions on the strength/value of individual resources work well. For example, as the resources are introduced, use of a graphic organizer on the overhead projector will help elicit which sources would work best to answer questions connected with the assignment. Students might prioritize resources and indicate the search strategy on a timeline (figure 3-4).

Figure 3-4 Presentation of Plan of Action: Third-Grade—Animal Habitat Project

---

Resources presented for whole class discussion and evaluation
Where do I begin?

| Electronic Encyclopedia | C-D ROM Mammals |
| Textbook | Science Encyclopedia |

Timeline: Nine days

Using the resources listed above, plan your research. Then plan your work time to cover making the diorama, and writing your paragraph and poem. In your journal, keep a log to record your reflections on how useful each resource is. You may revise your timeline if you need to, but be sure to discuss it with the teacher first.

Figure 3-5 Presentation of Plan of Action: Tenth-Grade—Literary Criticism

---

Rating Resources in Developing a Strategy

Resources	Look First	Most Productive

At the high school level, the suggested reference books are initially introduced by the assignment and *where to look first*. As the students work on the assignment, they keep a log that relates the actual usefulness of the resources, indicating which are *most productive* (see headings in figure 3-5). This process may be as simple as making check marks or as complicated as a learning log that includes reflective questions the students may have pertaining to seeking further information. Part of the project for high school students could include revisiting this original evaluation of the sources when they get to Step 5 of the model and comparing that to the actual value they discovered as the plan was put into action.

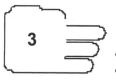

This is the doing-the-job step. In some respects, it is the hardest one to monitor. Clarifying questions include:

- Are all components of the assignment in evidence?
- Is the job progressing according to the timeline?
- Is my plan of action working?

This is where the students are truly working out the plan of action. It includes doing the actual locating and accessing of information; taking notes; outlining the project all the way to the rough drafts. Although much of the model can be worked through as an entire class, it is at this step that the students must become independent about their work. The teacher and LMS are more facilitators at this point.

As teacher and LMS are now mainly observers, developing an observation checklist would be helpful. Deadlines for specific components such as note cards, bibliographies, outlines, and rough drafts also help to keep the students on task. As time allows, individual conferencing on the projects insures the students are on the right track. Conferencing also offers an opportunity to see that the students' work is reflective of the actual assignment and in keeping with the plan of action. This is also the time to see if the plan of action needs to be modified for better success. Figures 3-6 and 3-7 are examples of documentation for this step.

Figure 3-6 Presentation of Let's Do the Job: Third-Grade—Animal Habitat Project

Checklist for Plan of Action

Following Timeline	Yes No	Comments
Day One		
Day Two		
Day Three		
Day Four		
Day Five		
Day Six		
Day Seven		
Day Eight		
Day Nine		

Figure 3-7 Presentation of Let's Do the Job: Tenth-Grade English—Literary Criticism

Deadlines for Specific Components

Due	Requirement	Date Turned In	Points Received
10-29	1 bib card, 1 note card		
11-1	5 note cards		
11-3	4 bib cards		
11-5	research complete		
11-6	outline		
11-8	rough draft		
11-12	works cited page		
11-19	final draft		
11-20	evaluation of process and product		

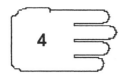

This step may take a variety of forms. Depending on the assignment, the finished product may be written or oral; a demonstration; an illustration; or a multimedia presentation, to name just a few. It is important to present the expectations for the finished product in the initial assignment. Use these clarifying questions to help the students determine if they have done their best work:

- Does the product reflect the specific parameters of the assignment?
- Does the quality reflect the students' best efforts?
- Has the finished product been reviewed by a peer, parent and/or teacher for ideas for improvement?

Just as there are many forms that the finished product may take, so are there infinite ways to assess the product. For the teacher and LMS, specific grading criteria should have been conveyed at the time of the assignment. For example, if spelling and grammar count, that must be made clear from the beginning; it isn't fair to change the rules later. One of the best assessment instruments is a rubric that covers the specific criteria the instructor feels contribute to the overall grade.

At the elementary level, the rubric may be as simple as a checklist indicating that all components of the assignment are in evidence. As students become more familiar with this method of assessment, qualitative rubrics will give the students a clearer picture of their accomplishments. Upper elementary and middle school students are capable of self-evaluation. Particularly useful are those self-evaluation rubrics which the students have helped design. Figure 3-8 is an example of a rubric for the elementary level.

Peer evaluation is helpful at the high school level. The quality of the peer evaluation could become a component of the assignment reflecting the ability of the student doing the evaluation as well as the student receiving the evaluation. Figure 3-9 is an example of a rubric incorporating peer review at the high school level.

Figure 3-8 Presentation of Product Evaluation: Third-Grade—Animal Habitat Project

Scoring Rubric for Finished Product # indicates points given for each component Grading Scale: A = 23-25; B = 20-22; C = 16-19; D = 14-15; F = 0-13					
1. Competency Test	1	2	3	4	5
Chapter 11					
Chapter 12					
2. Diorama	1	2	3	4	5
Labeled food, space, shelter, water					
3. Four-Line Poem	1	2	3	4	5
Rhyming words					
Word processing					
4. Food Web Paragraph	1	2	3	4	5
Five sentences					
Organization					
Word processing					
5. Quality work	1	2	3	4	5
Neatly done					
Worked independently					
Completed on time					

Figure 3-9 Presentation of Product Evaluation: Tenth-Grade English—Literary Criticism

Scoring Rubric for Product Evaluation Using the Following Point Value:

1 — ineffective

2 — moderately effective

3 — effective

4 — highly effective

(Students fill one out on their own product; the teacher also fills one out.)

_____ 1. Does the paper focus on the excellences and deficiencies of one or more of the following: style, theme, literary influence, character portrayal, point of view, truth, affirmative-
ness, force, vitality, beauty, imagery, tone, symmetry, idea, logic, or probability?

_____ 2. Does the paper stick with the thematic purpose identified in the introduction?

_____ 3. Does the body of the paper contain principal points that support and illustrate the
thematic purpose?

_____ 4. Does the paper avoid describing or retelling of the work?

_____ 5. Does the paper avoid looking at the parts to the exclusion of the whole?

The evaluation step is perhaps the one most overlooked. The finished
product has been turned in; a grade has been given. If the students are to
apply all that they have learned, then it becomes critical to go beyond the
finished product and ask these questions:

- Did I do all of the work to fulfill the assignment?
- Was my plan of action adequate?
- Did I do my best quality work?
- What have I learned?
- How does the finished product demonstrate what I have learned?
- What will I do differently the next time?

One of the best ways to achieve step 5 at every level is simply to brainstorm with the entire
class on how the project went. This allows all students to contribute freely without fear of reper-
cussion. Often the teacher and LMS will discover where they might change and/or improve certain aspects of the assignment the next time. For example, the assignment might need more
clarification, perhaps there were insufficient sources available or the time frame was too short.

For a more tangible documentation, elementary students could write one, two, or three
things they learned from doing this assignment, such as in figure 3-10. Middle and high school
students could write a reflective paragraph about what they have learned and how they will apply that knowledge the next time (figure 3-11).

Once the model has been implemented with a class, the steps should be posted in a permanent, highly visible location. On subsequent projects, the teacher or LMS may only have to ask a question that jogs the students into reflecting which step they are on to get their thinking in focus. It is important to stress the interrelationships of all the steps: does the product reflect the requirements of the assignment? Does the plan of action represent the best use of materials and resources available? Is the student transferring knowledge gained from one project to the next? Do the rubrics measure the intended objectives? Is quality work the outcome?

Visuals that keep the steps of the model in front of the students help to make the process a part of every day language. Figure 3-12 shows the model in its entirety and creates a basis for a poster. The secondary level students may not appreciate a "hand" analogy, so a bulleted version works just as well (figure 3-13). Bookmarks with the steps and parameter questions are also helpful (figure 3-14 for elementary, figure 3-15 for middle school/high school).

Figure 3-10 Presentation of Process Evaluation: Third-Grade—Animal Habitat Unit

---

Third-Grade—Animal Habitat Unit
Evaluation Checklist and Reflection

	Yes	No
Did my plan work?	_____	_____
Did I do my best work?	_____	_____

I am really proud of my diorama because:

Other people (parents, peers, or teachers) said my project was:

Figure 3-11 Presentation of Process Evaluation: Tenth-Grade English—Literary Criticism

---

Process Evaluation — Reflection

1. Did writing a description of the assignment (Step 1) help you to better understand what you needed to do?

2. Did developing a research strategy prior to beginning the research help you organize the search: save you time and/or frustration (Step 2)? Why?

3. Did having specific dates and points awarded for each step of the process help you keep on task?

4. What have you discovered using this process that will help you in your next assignment?

SUMMARY

The model provides a problem-solving method for students as well as a planning tool for teachers and LMSs. The Handy 5 offers the integrated problem-solving model in easily understood terminology for students. Use of the clarifying questions helps to cement the students' understanding of each step. Assessments for some steps may be simple checklists or logs while other steps may need more detailed rubrics. Constant reinforcement of the Handy 5 gives the student an invaluable tool, one that is available every day.

Examples of the unit outlines described in this chapter are found in Chapter 9, along with other examples of completed unit plans.

REFERENCES

American Association of School Librarians and Association for Educational Communications and Technology. *Information Power: Building Partnerships for Learning.* Chicago: American Library Association, 1998.

Figure 3-12 Elementary Poster (*Toolkit CD*-Posters)

The Handy 5

What am I supposed to do?
- **What is the assignment?**
- **What is the time schedule?**
- **What new terms are there?**
- **What should the end product look like?**

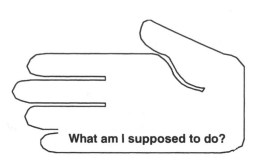

How do I get the job done?
- **What resources will I need?**
- **Where should I look first?**
- **Which sources give me the best or most information?**
- **How will I evaluate them?**

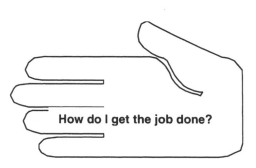

Let's do the job!
- **Are all the pieces of the assignment in place?**
- **Is the job progressing according to the timeline?**

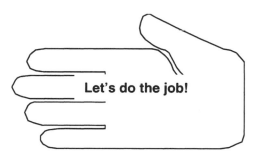

What do I have to show for it?
- **Does the product reflect the guidelines of the assignment?**
- **Is this my best quality work?**

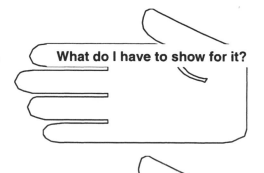

How well did I do?
- **What have I learned?**
- **How does the finished product demonstrate this?**
- **What will I do differently next time?**

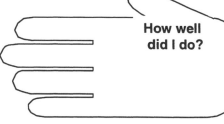

Figure 3-13 Middle School/High School Poster (*Toolkit CD*-Posters)

The Handy 5

1. What am I supposed to do?
- What are the guidelines?
- What is the time schedule?
- What new terms are there?
- What questions do I need to answer?
- What should the end product look like?

2. How do I get the job done?
- What resources will I need?
- Where should I look first?
- Which sources give me the best or most answers?
- How will I evaluate the usefulness of the resources?

3. Let's do the job!
- Are all of the pieces of the assignment in place?
- Is the job progressing according to the timeline?

4. What do I have to show for it?
- Does the product reflect the specific guidelines of the assignment?
- Before turning in my work, have I had someone else check it and offer ideas for improvement?

5. How well did I do?
- What have I learned?
- How does the finished product demonstrate this?
- What will I do differently next time?

Figure 3-14 Elementary Bookmark (*Toolkit CD*-Bookmark–Passes)

The Handy 5

What am I supposed to do?
- **What is the assignment?**
- **What is the time schedule?**
- **What new terms are there?**
- **What should the end product look like?**

How do I get the job done?
- **What resources will I need?**
- **Where should I look first?**
- **Which sources give me the best or most information?**
- **How will I evaluate them?**

Let's do the job!
- **Are all the pieces of the assignment in place?**
- **Is the job progressing according to the timeline?**

What do I have to show for it?
- **Does the product reflect the guidelines of the assignment?**
- **Is this my best quality work?**

How well did I do?
- **What have I learned?**
- **How does the finished product demonstrate this?**
- **What will I do differently next time?**

Developed by Betsy Losey & Shelia Blume

The Handy 5

What am I supposed to do?
- **What is the assignment?**
- **What is the time schedule?**
- **What new terms are there?**
- **What should the end product look like?**

How do I get the job done?
- **What resources will I need?**
- **Where should I look first?**
- **Which sources give me the best or most information?**
- **How will I evaluate them?**

Let's do the job!
- **Are all the pieces of the assignment in place?**
- **Is the job progressing according to the timeline?**

What do I have to show for it?
- **Does the product reflect the guidelines of the assignment?**
- **Is this my best quality work?**

How well did I do?
- **What have I learned?**
- **How does the finished product demonstrate this?**
- **What will I do differently next time?**

Developed by Betsy Losey & Shelia Blume

Figure 3-15 Middle School/High School Bookmark (*Toolkit CD*-Bookmark–Passes)

The Handy 5

What am I supposed to do?
- **What are the guidelines?**
- **What is the time schedule?**
- **What new terms are there?**
- **What questions do I need to answer?**
- **What should the end product look like?**

How do I get the job done?
- **What resources will I need?**
- **Where should I look first?**
- **Which sources give me the best or most information?**
- **How will I evaluate them?**

Let's do the job!
- **Are all the pieces of the assignment in place?**
- **Is the job progressing according to the time line?**

What do I have to show for it?
- **Does the product reflect the specific guidelines of the assignment?**
- **Before turning in my work, have I had someone else check it and offer ideas for improvement?**

How well did I do?
- **What have I learned?**
- **How does the finished product demonstrate this?**
- **What will I do differently next time?**

Developed by Carol Fox

The Handy 5

What am I supposed to do?
- **What are the guidelines?**
- **What is the time schedule?**
- **What new terms are there?**
- **What questions do I need to answer?**
- **What should the end product look like?**

How do I get the job done?
- **What resources will I need?**
- **Where should I look first?**
- **Which sources give me the best or most information?**
- **How will I evaluate them?**

Let's do the job!
- **Are all the pieces of the assignment in place?**
- **Is the job progressing according to the time line?**

What do I have to show for it?
- **Does the product reflect the specific guidelines of the assignment?**
- **Before turning in my work, have I had someone else check it and offer ideas for improvement?**

How well did I do?
- **What have I learned?**
- **How does the finished product demonstrate this?**
- **What will I do differently next time?**

Developed by Carol Fox

4

Using the Model at the Primary Level: The Handy 3

Introducing the Handy 3 Primary Model

The Colorful Handy 3 Model

Collaborative Planning and the Handy 3

Resources Developed to Teach the Model

Summary

INTRODUCING THE HANDY 3 PRIMARY MODEL

The Handy 5 has proven to be a highly useful tool for teacher collaboration, an effective lesson-designing tool and a method of approach for students when they are completing an assignment, project, or presentation. In the upper elementary library media program, the process of the Handy 5 may be the subject of the lesson itself.

The five-step model is taught in the upper elementary grades; however, it is reduced to three steps for students in kindergarten, first, and early second grade. The use of color for the individual steps in the model in addition to a variety of lesson materials and strategies make the introduction of the Handy 3 model an exciting experience for elementary students.

The basic elements of the Handy 3 model are introduced to pre-readers and early readers when the students begin to develop and understand the idea of sequence. Students recognize that the story has a development of sequences from beginning, middle, and end. The Handy 3 model is presented in conjunction with the plot of a book or story, and it becomes the framework for the Handy 5 presentation series of lessons, moving the students into the research process.

Strategies and resources have been developed to introduce the Handy 3 model. Each Handy 3 concept that is taught is strengthened with the use of puppets, posters, bookmarks, story sequence cards, and other memory devices to aid in the understanding of each step of the problem-solving process. These strategies and supplemental resources promote the understanding of the Handy 3 model in a dynamic and sequential manner.

THE COLORFUL HANDY 3 MODEL: USING COLOR TO CHANGE EMOTIONAL STATES IN THE HANDY 3

An effort has been made to simplify the model for the early reader, students in kindergarten, first, and second grades. The problem-solving process has been condensed to three steps. By adding colors to the presentation, the steps are visually reinforced and defined for the primary student. Also, the use of colors helps change the student's emotional state and signals to the brain that new learning is taking place. The colors chosen for the Handy 3 have an established environmental association with the colors in a traffic signal light. The meaning commonly associated with the color is applied to the three steps in the Handy 3.

The first step in the Handy 3 is assigned the color yellow. The color yellow signals caution; and the student considers possible solutions to the problem and how to solve it. The second step is paired with the color green. This is the step that requires action. It is time to get going and test the strategies developed earlier. The color red is used for the final step in The Handy 3 Primary Model. This indicates that it is time to stop and evaluate the strategies used to solve the problem. Did they work? Could it have been accomplished in another way? Figure 4-1 illustrates the outline of the model as it is used in conjunction with a story. It indicates the portion of the story being discussed, the color assigned to the step, the cue to the student and finally the questions that are reviewed after the story has been presented.

Figure 4-1 The Handy 3 Primary Model Outline

THE HANDY 3 PRIMARY MODEL

1. THE BEGINNING (yellow)
What am I supposed to do?
What problem does the main character have to solve?

2. THE MIDDLE (green)
Let's do the job
What will the main character do to solve the problem?

3. THE END (red)
How well did I do?
Do you think that the main character came up with a good solution?

COLLABORATIVE PLANNING AND THE HANDY 3

When the LMS and the classroom teacher work together to plan the Handy 3 lesson, the regular planning template and explanation found in chapter 6 will still be useful. There might be some adjustments however. Usually the assignment will be a simple activity to be completed in one or two periods under the directed teaching of the LMS or the classroom teacher and so students don't need to re-state the assignment or show they understand it to the extent that older students will. On the planning template, the assignment might be a simple statement relating what the activity is to accomplish. Rather than the students being concerned with choosing the appropriate strategy for fulfilling the assignment in step 2, the teacher will simply teach the strategy needed or model the activity. Doing the job is the activity, the purpose of the lesson. Some activities will lend themselves to having the students assess the correctness of the activity or the product. Others may not and it becomes the teacher's responsibility to judge whether the activity was successful. More effort will be put into helping the student reflect on the activity and seeing how it might be used again. While collaboration is still the ultimate goal in planning and teaching, it might not always work as completely with the Handy 3. The LMS might work more in a support role in re-enforcing literature strategies learned in the classroom.

RESOURCES DEVELOPED TO TEACH THE MODEL

Simplified sets of materials are important to the presentation of the Handy 3 and can be easily adapted from materials found in other chapters in this book.

The variety of resources used for the delivery of the Handy 3 is an important aspect of the presentation of the model. The materials add a dynamic and interesting quality to the lesson, while assisting in the comprehension and retention of the Handy 3.

The introduction of the problem-solving model is usually paired with a short story. The student will follow the main character through the problem-solving process. The materials help the student review and understand each step of the model. The following materials are the basic resources that can be created to present the Handy 3 lessons.

THE HANDY 3 GRAPHIC ORGANIZER

The introduction of the primary problem-solving model is a resource used by the instructor and is paired with the presentation of a short story. The student follows the main character through the problem-solving process. The Handy 3 is introduced to students as soon as they understand the idea of story sequencing. Story sequencing with the Handy 3 graphic organizer is used for reviewing and arranging a series of picture cards into the logical order to create the story from beginning to end. An example of a story sequence exercise using the Handy 3 graphic organizer is shown in figure 4-2. This example uses the story *"Let's Get a Pup!" Said Kate* by Bob Graham. The rectangle sections are used to record a short summary, draw a sketch of the action or an area to place a picture card from the story. Each individual hand is outlined with the appropriate color to assist in reinforcing the sequential steps of the Handy 3 model. When using a story to teach the model, the student has a chance to envision the main character as the problem-solver. Students retell the story by placing the picture cards in the appropriate order or sequence on the graphic organizer. This resource can be illustrated on a dry-erase board or made into a large bulletin board for a working display. The chart or bulletin board display changes when a new story is presented to the class. Figure 4-6 is a blank form to be adapted for personal use.

Figure 4-2 The Handy 3 Primary Model Graphic Organizer

The Handy 3 Primary Model Graphic Organizer

Graphic Organizer for *"Let's Get a Pup!" Said Kate* by Bob Graham

- What am I supposed to do?
  Question
  What is the problem that the main character needs to solve?

Answer
Kate would like to know how to find a new pet dog to live with the family. (Picture card depicts Kate running down the hallway to her parents' bedroom to ask them for a new dog.)

- Get the job done.
  Question
  What is the main character doing to solve the problem?

Answer
Kate and her family spent a lot of time talking about what kind of dog that they would like to get. They read the newspaper and looked in the ads to locate a dog. They visit a local rescue center and adopted a dog. (Picture cards show a variety of actions taken by Kate and her family as they search for a new dog.)

- How well did I do?
  Questions
  How well did the character do the job?
  What could he or she have done differently?

Answer
Kate and her family did an excellent job finding a new dog. They looked at all kinds of dogs at the rescue center. Maybe Kate could have adopted just one animal and then she might have been able to adopt a cat, too! (Picture cards reveal Kate sitting on the couch with the dogs while reading a book.)

THE HANDY 3 PRIMARY POSTER

The poster can be used in several ways. Reproduce the poster found in figure 4-7 by copying on white chart paper and enlarging to the desired size for display in the library or the classroom. Copy the hand portion of the poster onto yellow, red, and green construction paper. The construction paper hand will be the exact match of the hand on the black and white poster. As each step is introduced in the lesson, add the construction paper hand to the poster. Place the picture card that depicts the action in the story next to the appropriate step of the Handy 3. Display the poster and the picture cards on a bulletin board. Students enjoy reviewing the story using this poster. It helps them to remember the order of events and details of the story when retelling it to a friend. As students grow in their understanding of the problem-solving process, the remaining steps can be added to the complete poster of the Handy 5 model. The language of the steps in the primary poster has been kept the same as the Handy 5; however, the language may be modified to fit the grade level of the students involved.

THE HANDY 3 PRIMARY BOOKMARK

This resource in figure 4-8 is an adaptation of the Handy 5 elementary poster. It is resized to allow two eleven-inch tall bookmarks to fit on a single 8½" x 11" page. It can be modified to include one simple question, draw a small picture, or write a few words under each step. Revise it to fit the needs of the students so that it is appropriate for the story review or an assignment. When using it during a story-review lesson, the student should have this resource while the story is read aloud. The student is instructed to write down a brief remark or sentence about the main character as they progress through the three-step process. The instructor may stop the story to review what the main character is doing at each step of the problem-solving process. This is a great resource to use when checking for understanding during the lesson. It can also be used as a table activity and enlarged as a full-page worksheet. Younger students can cut out miniature story sequence cards and glue them next to the appropriate step.

The bookmark can also be adapted for use as a hall pass for the library. The bookmark and hall pass share an 8½" x 11" sheet of construction paper as seen in figure 4-8. It can be laminated for an environmentally friendly resource. The teacher fills out the hall pass portion and the student fills in the first step of the Handy 3 before arriving in the library. When the student arrives in the library, the pass is reviewed and initialed by the librarian. Information can be recorded under the appropriate step to indicate the progress of the student when researching or working on an assignment. Students return to the classroom with evidence of their assignment progress. This is a great communication tool for the teacher, librarian, and student to share information about the nature of the library visit, the suggested length of the visit, and to record student's hallway travel time. The Handy 3 bookmark and hall pass resource is a helpful organizational tool to use when gathering information and completing an assignment or research project in the library media center.

TEACHER MODEL BOOK

Use the same open hands on the Handy 3 elementary poster (figure 4-7). They may be enlarged and printed on colored cardstock and used as a model for the lesson instruction when introducing the student handbook. The hands can also be used as the template for a large bulletin board display. When using this resource to make the bulletin board display, print them on construction paper in the colors selected for The Handy 3 Primary Model. Number each step of the model. Print out the questions for each step on large card stock. Place the questions below the corresponding hand for that step. The hands can be arranged in a vertical or horizontal array on the wall or bulletin board. Figure 4-9 shows the teacher model book.

STUDENT HANDBOOK

Each page of the student handbook includes a working page for each step of the Handy 3. It is a place for the early or non-reader to draw the main character in action as the main character works to solve a problem in the story. As the story is read aloud, the students may draw scenes from the story on the appropriate Handy 3 page. Questions are included in the student workbook to assist the teacher as students retell the story. The handbook can be used to reinforce important concepts such as vocabulary development, story order, main character, and the parts of a book. See figure 4-10 for samples of the student workbook that can be reproduced to fit on an 8½" x 11" or a 12" x 18" page.

"HANDY" PUPPET

The glove puppet is a resource developed to review the steps of the Handy 5. It can be used to present the Handy 3 as well. Each character on the glove has a personality that corresponds to the steps of the model. When presenting the Handy 3 model, skip the second and fourth puppet on the hand. Tell the students that those characters will have a lot more to say when they use the model in the third, fourth, and fifth grade.

The puppet is used to demonstrate to the students that each step or character works together to solve the problem. Give each character a personality and appearance guided by the information presented in each step of the Handy 3. When making the glove puppet, distinguish the Handy 3 characters with longer yarn hair or larger wiggle eyes to make them stand out from the rest of the characters on the glove. During the puppet presentation, each puppet wiggles as it speaks, with the fingers fully extended. This reinforces the sequential aspect of the problem-solving process and avoids any embarrassing gestures with the puppet.

As an alternative to the Handy 5 finger puppet, consider using a three-fingered puppet. Design it to resemble a three-toed dinosaur. Use a favorite dinosaur story and show how the main dinosaur character uses the three-step process of problem solving.

Figure 4-3 "Handy" Puppet

Developed by JK Stover

STORY HAND

This resource is a large outline of an open hand. The large hand can be illustrated on a large sheet of paper or on a dry-erase board. When using a large sheet of paper, make sure that when the hand is folded in half it will fit in a laminating machine. When laminated it becomes a reusable resource for another presentation. It can be used again when another story is read aloud to the class, by inserting appropriate story sequence cards.

The Story Hand is used in conjunction with a short story or book. Print out sequence cards from the story. The pictures are selected from the story and illustrate key events. Post the pictures on the wall near the Story Hand. As the story is being read aloud to the class, ask the students to assist in selecting and placing the picture cards on the steps or fingers on the Story Hand. The center palm portion of the hand is used to record the title and the author of the story being used in the model. The large Story Hand can be posted on the wall as a poster and used as a reminder of the sequence of the story and the problem-solving process. It also makes a great demonstration model when used in conjunction with the graphic organizer (figure 4-6). This model can be useful to transition primary students to the use of the Handy 5 model.

Figure 4-4 The Story Hand Shown as a Transitional Model for the Handy 5 Presentation

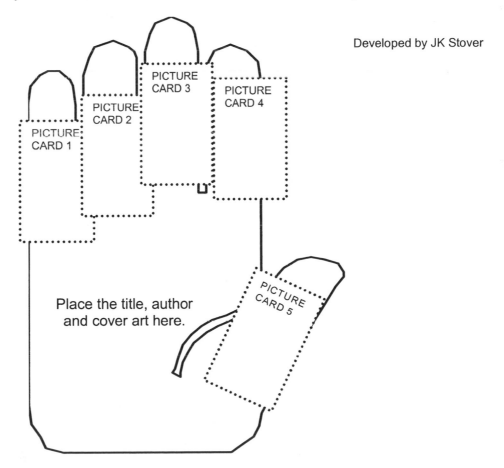

Developed by JK Stover

HANDY 3 ENGINE AND BOXCARS

This was developed for the pre-reader and supplements the Handy 3. The model resembles a short train. The engine portion of the model can be a basket, tub, or folder that holds the materials needed for the lesson. The yellow, green, and red boxcars hold the story sequence picture cards. The boxcars may be baskets or file folders used in an interactive bulletin board display.

The students select and sort the story picture cards into the color-coded boxcars as the story is read aloud to the class. The librarian or teacher can move the picture cards to the appropriate basket or folder and also discuss story elements such as title, author, illustrator, main character, and story order. Use the Handy 3 vocabulary to guide the discussion. It is helpful when presenting the Handy 3 Engine and Boxcars to choose a book that uses a train as the main character in the story.

Figure 4-5 Handy 3 Engine and Boxcars

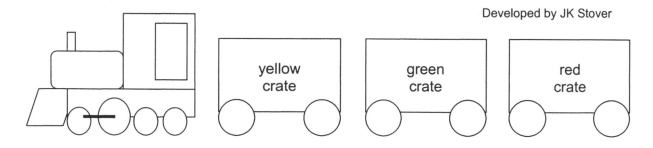

Developed by JK Stover

HANDY 3 PAGE MARKERS

When preparing the class to begin a more careful examination of the actions of the problem-solving character in a story, use a color-coded page marker to indicate the correlation to the Handy 3 step. After the Handy 3 has been reviewed, a story is shared with the class. While reading the story to the class the teacher applies a self-stick page marker to the appropriate page in the story. The self-stick marker indicates where the student can find a picture that represents the Handy 3 step. The story does not stop when the page marker is applied. It is used as a guide to assist students in the Handy 3 review process and the retelling of the story. It is also helpful as a checking device when comparing the order of the picture cards to the order of the events in the story.

CONNECTIONS WITH LITERATURE

The process of selecting a book that will help explain the Handy 3 problem-solving process has several key components. Choose a high interest book that has a clear sequence. Make sure that the book chosen for the kindergarten level has a single or main character that appears on every page. The storyline and the illustrations should show the main character discovering a problem, and deciding how to solve the problem. The story should also show the main character enjoying, regretting, or refining the solution to the problem. The story should demonstrate several choices that the character makes to arrive at the solution to the problem. Finally, do not forget humor. It is important to face a problem with a balance of humor and determination. With all of these elements included, your search will be successful when looking for a book to showcase the Handy 3. It will include examples of the main character working to solve a problem in a creative step-by-step approach. The following list of book titles will be helpful when planning Handy 3 lessons with the main character as the problem solver.

- *Arthur's Nose*, by Marc Brown (K-3)
- *Picky Mrs. Pickle*, by Christine Schneider (1-3)
- *Widget*, by Lyn Rossiter McFarland (K-2)
- *Peanut's Emergency*, by Cristina Salat (K-2)
- *Miss Nelson Is Missing*, by Harry Allard (K-3)
- *The Hallo-Wiener*, by Dav Pilkey (K-2)
- *The True Story of the 3 Little Pigs*, by Jon Scieszka (K-3)
- *I'm Not Invited*, by Diana Cain Blumenthal (K-2)
- *There's a Nightmare in My Closet*, Mercer Mayer (K-2)
- *Arthur's Thanksgiving*, Marc Brown (1-3)
- *A New Barker in the House*, Tomie dePaola

SUMMARY

The Handy 5 Model has been simplified for the early or pre-reader and becomes The Handy 3 Primary Model. It incorporates fewer steps and uses color to visually define those steps. Strategies and materials have been developed or can be adapted from Handy 5 materials to support the lessons when introducing the model in the primary grades.

REFERENCES

Allard, Harry. *Miss Nelson Is Missing.* New York: Houghton Mifflin, 1991.

Brown, Marc. *Arthur's Nose. 25th Anniversary Limited Edition.* New York: Little Brown & Company, 2001.

Brown, Marc. *Arthur's Thanksgiving.* Boston: Little Brown & Company, 1983.

Blumenthal, Diana Cain. *I'm Not Invited.* New York: Atheneum Books for Young Readers, 2003.

dePaola, Tomie. *A New Barker in the House.* New York: Puffin Books, 2004.

Graham, Bob. *"Let's Get a Pup!" Said Kate.* Cambridge, MA: Candlewick Press, 2001.

Mayer, Mercer. *There's a Nightmare in My Closet.* New York: Dial Books for Young Readers, 1990.

McFarland, Lyn Rossiter. *Widget.* New York: Farrar, Straus & Giroux, 2006.

Pilkey, Dav. *The Hallo-Wiener.* New York: Scholastic Press, 1999.

Salat, Christina. *Peanut's Emergency.* Watertown, MA: Whispering Coyote, 2002.

Schneider, Christine. *Picky Mrs. Pickle.* New York: Walker and Co., 1999.

Scieszka, Jon. *The True Story of the 3 Little Pigs.* New York: Viking, 1999.

Figure 4-6 Handy 3 Graphic Organizer (*Toolkit CD*-Miscellaneous)

▪ What am I supposed to do?   Developed by JK Stover
Question
What is the problem that the main character needs to solve?

▪ Get the job done.
Question
What is the main character doing to solve the problem?

▪ How well did I do?
Questions
How well did the character do the job?
What could he or she have done differently?

Figure 4-7 Handy 3 Poster (*Toolkit CD*-Posters)

The Handy 3

What am I supposed to do?
- **What is the assignment?**
- **What is the time schedule?**
- **What new terms are there?**
- **What should the end product look like?**

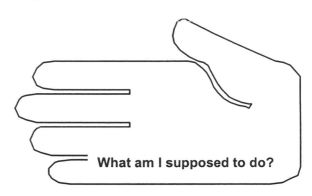

Let's get the job done!
- **Are all the pieces of the assignment in place?**
- **Is the job progressing according to the timeline?**

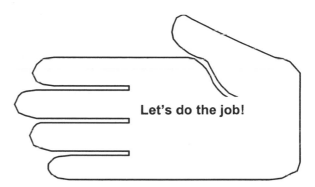

How well did I do?
- **What have I learned?**
- **How does the finished product demonstrate this?**
- **What will I do differently next time?**

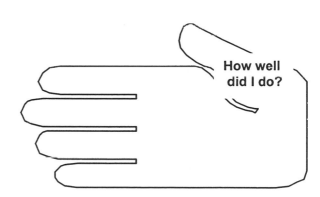

Developed by Betsy Losey

Figure 4-8 Primary Bookmark (*Toolkit CD*-Bookmark–Posters)

The Handy 3 Model

Figure 4-9 Teacher Model Book

1 **WHAT AM I SUPPOSED TO DO?**
Question: What is the problem that the main character needs to solve? What is the assignment?
Answer:

2 **LET'S DO THE JOB.**
Question: What is the main character doing to solve the problem? What will I need to do to get the assignment done?
Answer:

3 **HOW WELL DID I DO?**
Question: How well did the character do the job? What could they have done differently? What could I have done differently with this assignment?
Answer:

Developed by JK Stover

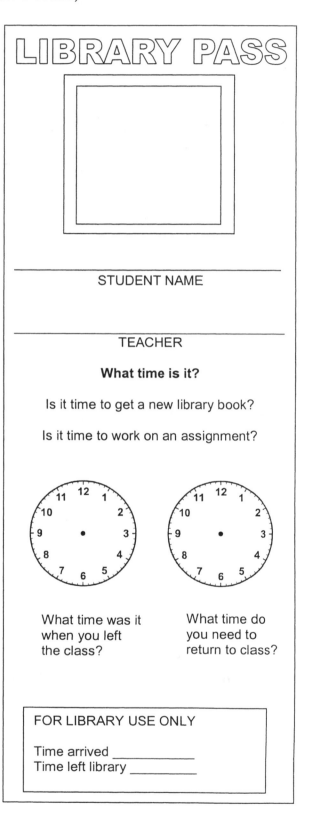

Figure 4-9 Teacher Model Handbook (*Toolkit CD*-Student–Teacher Handbook)

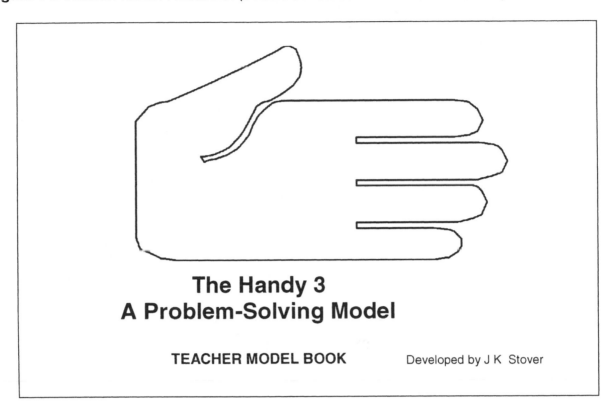

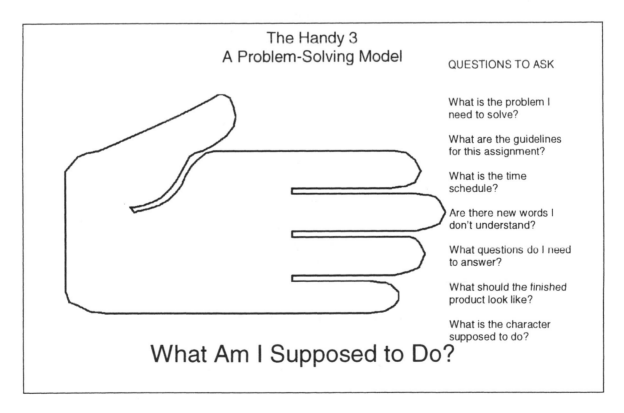

Figure 4-9 (continued) Teacher Model Handbook

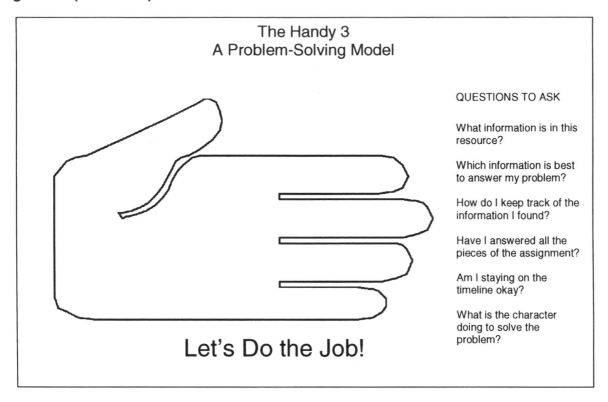

The Handy 3
A Problem-Solving Model

QUESTIONS TO ASK

What information is in this resource?

Which information is best to answer my problem?

How do I keep track of the information I found?

Have I answered all the pieces of the assignment?

Am I staying on the timeline okay?

What is the character doing to solve the problem?

Let's Do the Job!

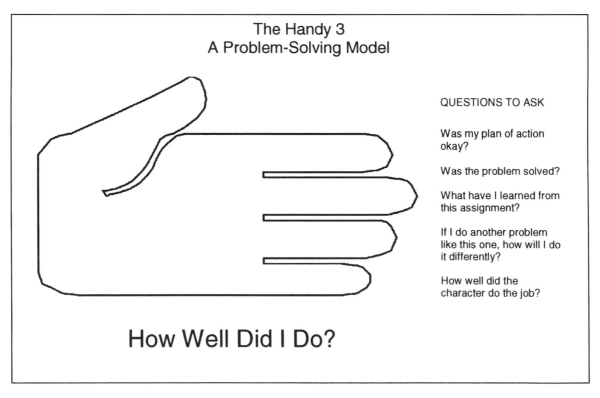

The Handy 3
A Problem-Solving Model

QUESTIONS TO ASK

Was my plan of action okay?

Was the problem solved?

What have I learned from this assignment?

If I do another problem like this one, how will I do it differently?

How well did the character do the job?

How Well Did I Do?

Figure 4-10 Student Handbook (*Toolkit CD*-Student–Teacher Handbook)

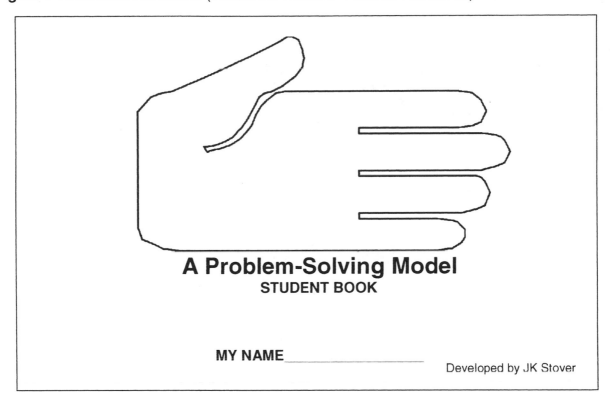

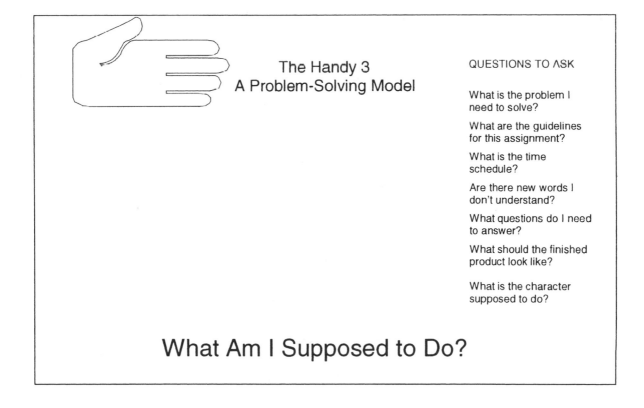

Figure 4-10 (continued) Student Handbook

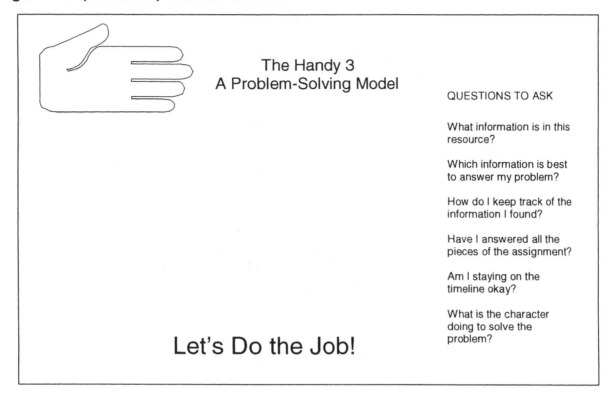

The Handy 3
A Problem-Solving Model

QUESTIONS TO ASK

What information is in this resource?

Which information is best to answer my problem?

How do I keep track of the information I found?

Have I answered all the pieces of the assignment?

Am I staying on the timeline okay?

What is the character doing to solve the problem?

Let's Do the Job!

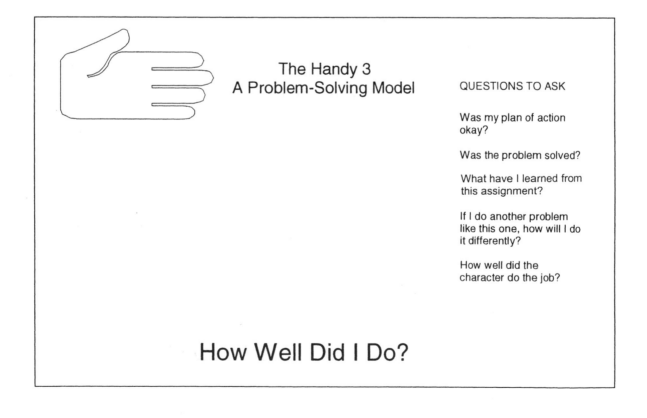

The Handy 3
A Problem-Solving Model

QUESTIONS TO ASK

Was my plan of action okay?

Was the problem solved?

What have I learned from this assignment?

If I do another problem like this one, how will I do it differently?

How well did the character do the job?

How Well Did I Do?

5

Applying the Handy 5 in the Classroom

Jigsaw Puzzle

Literature

Instructional Strategies for Each Step

STRATEGIES FOR APPLYING THE HANDY 5 IN THE CLASSROOM

Most of the time the Handy 5 model is presented as one big piece and it is thought that this is the only way it can be used. Research and subsequent use indicates that many small steps must be taught first before a big project incorporating all 5 steps can happen successfully.

An LMS or classroom teacher will already be familiar with many of the strategies that are suggested in this chapter. Dividing these strategies by the Handy 5 steps will help identify the best place for their use.

One of the first things to be considered is how to introduce the model to the students. In chapter 3 the Handy 5 kid talk was introduced. There were some suggestions for applying the model in the real world. But students need to understand and internalize the model so that it is indeed handy in classroom situations.

When first introducing the model to students, do a fairly straight-on explanation of the model and the parameters as outlined in chapter 3. Show how the fingers or the bulleted lists work to help students remember the steps and the questions to be asked for each. Make up bookmarks for students to carry with them that list the steps. Make posters to have in the library, the school hallway, and in the classrooms. Explain how the model can either work with an assignment as simple as answering the questions at the end of the chapter, with all of the information in the preceding text, or be a large project that can take several weeks and many steps to complete. The next stage would be to use the steps in a simple activity. Making trail mix would be one example. By using a variety of ingredients—M&Ms, peanuts, cereal, dried fruit, for example—students locate the ingredients, mix them according to a set recipe, and then assess their work. Another example would be having the students put together a simple jigsaw puzzle.

Teaching the Handy 5 Using Jigsaw Puzzles

This activity is a fun way to reinforce the Handy 5 after introducing the steps and talking about the purpose for each step. It is probably best used with 3-5 graders.

Supplies for each group
- 1 puzzle with very few, large pieces per group
- Sealable bag for each puzzle
- Scrap paper and pencil for each group

• 2 pieces of colored paper, 1 about 2 x 2 ", another 4 x 4 " folded in half to make a table tent

Procedures
• Code the back of each puzzle piece with a colored dot (magic marker).
• Take the puzzle pieces out of the box and put in the sealable plastic bag. Put a to 2 x 2 square of paper on the outside of the bag that corresponds to the colored dot on the puzzle piece.
• Place the larger table tent on each group table.
• Take one puzzle piece from about half of the puzzles and place the extra pieces in the remaining boxes. (The idea is for some puzzles to be short one piece and others have one too many pieces).

First review the steps of the model using a bookmark or a poster. Use the suggested talking points below to take the class through the steps.

Step 1: The Assignment: What Am I Supposed to Do?

• Assignment is to put a puzzle together during library time.
• Work in groups and complete it today.
• Ask several questions about the assignment and have students indicate understanding by showing thumbs up thumbs down.

Step 2: Plan of Action: How Do I Get the Job Done?

• Choose a strategy for completing the assignment.
• Discuss and list ways of putting a puzzle together—sort by similar colors, separate by straight edges and corners, box picture.
• Discuss any other strategies.
• Explain class will not have the box picture to use today so must choose any other strategy from those listed.

Step 3: Let's Do the Job!

• Explain correlation between colored piece of paper on table and locating the sealable bag with a matching color around the library. (This is locating information).
• When each group has located puzzle pieces, they return to their table.
• Group puts puzzle together using chosen strategy.

Step 4: Product Evaluation: What Do I Have to Show for It?

• Allow students time to complete their puzzle.
• Discussion about any problems with the puzzle (too many, not enough pieces?).
• Discussion about fixing the problem of incorrect number of pieces (the assignment, go back for additional information, throw away information that does not answer the assignment).
• Students work on getting the right puzzle pieces to the right group in order to complete the picture.
• Discuss the fact that now the puzzle (assignment) is completed. Does it fit the criteria given in the assignment?

Step 5: Process Evaluation: How Well Did I Do?

- Discuss the steps of the process used in completing the assignment.
- Reflect on the processes used in this activity.
- Did everyone do the best they could?
- Did everyone work on the assignment?
- Was the group able to figure out what to do to fix the problem of too many, not enough puzzle pieces?
- What would make it easier to do this assignment another time? (Perhaps having the picture?)

TEACHING THE HANDY 5 USING LITERATURE

Another way to practice the steps of the model at first is the use of literature. Start with a picture book that demonstrates the model.

For example, read any version of *The Three Little Pigs* to the class. After reading the story, talk about whether the pigs had a plan when they left home. Had they given any thought to any part of the situation? About the only thing they really had was the assignment—Leave Home!

The three little pigs didn't use any selection of resources (building materials for their houses). They just took the first thing that came to them (the men walking down the road with a load of hay, sticks, or bricks). Using this story will show them the hazard of just taking the easy way out—using the first thing they think of with no planning at all. The pig with the bricks lucked out. Maybe the next time he won't be so lucky.

If you want to review the steps of the model before you begin a new unit, use a short fable by Aesop. The five steps become readily apparent.

Jan Stover from Highland Park Central Elementary in Topeka has used *Arthur's Thanksgiving* by Marc Brown as a way of introducing the Handy 5 to her students. Read the story and then discuss the following points.

Step 1: What am I supposed to do? Mr. Ratburn has chosen Arthur to direct the Thanksgiving play.

Step 2: How do I get the job done? Assign the parts. The narrator would have the biggest part, but the turkey would represent the spirit of Thanksgiving.

Step 3: Let's do the job! Arthur received many bribes from would-be actors, but he kept going back to steps 1-2. He was to direct the play and the actors had to meet certain criteria (narrator, turkey). He also had to schedule rehearsals and keep everyone on target, the best Thanksgiving play ever.

Step 4: What do I have to show for it? A successful play. After many problems the play is given to the rest of the school and it looks like it was a success.

Step 5: How well did I do? Arthur was successful. He put on a play that the rest of the school enjoyed. His classmates were still his friends.

Nate the Great and the Missing Key by Marjorie Sharmat would be fun to use with the lower grades as a review of the 5 steps. Prepare a sign for each step of the model on tag board strips.

Fasten the strips to popsicle stick or dowel rods. As the story is read, have the student with the appropriate sign hold it up when the part of the story that demonstrates a step is read.

Step 1: What am I supposed to do? Find the key to Annie's house

Step 2: How do I get the job done? "Tell me about your key."
Left it on the table when I went to get food for Fang.
Rosamond and cats were there.
Rosamond left, locked the house and left a poem.
Who else has a key?

Step 3: Let's do the job! Searching for the key
Went to Annie's house.
Got a description of the key.
Looked for all the places a key could be hidden—Annie's house, Oliver's house, bank, garbage cans.

> **Your key can be found
> At a place that is round
> A place that is safe
> And where things are shiny.
> A place that is big
> Because it's not tiny.
> And this is a poem
> And I went home.**

Step 4: What do I have to show for it? Located the key on Fang's collar. It was round, big and safe and found where things are shiny.

Step 5: How well did I do? I did well because I found the key. I wanted to talk to Rosamond about her choice. I had to sit next to Fang at the party because I'd solved the case.

INSTRUCTIONAL STRATEGIES FOR TEACHING THE INDIVIDUAL 5 STEPS

During the research phase of the Handy 5 model, it was discovered that most of the time students benefited from working on the steps one or two at a time. This is particularly true when the model is just being introduced. Use of the puzzle, or some other method, is necessary to show the whole process, but then individual steps need to be addressed. Only one or two complete 5-step projects per class would be expected in a school year.

LMSs have developed a host of lessons to help teach the traditional "library skills." Even when doing collaborative planning and teaching there is still a need for teaching those kinds of skills. Instead of re-inventing lessons, just think about what the main focus of the lesson is and it will probably fit the specific skills needed to teach one of the 5 steps of the model.

Step 1: The Assignment

Students must learn to question what the assignment is. Only by fully understanding the assignment and all of its parameters can a student be certain of success.

- Fill out assignment planner part 1 (figure 5-1).
- List the specific pieces of the assignment.
- Discuss what the final product might look like. Have good and bad models to share.
- Share the pieces of the assignment with a shoulder partner.
- Respond to oral questions with thumbs up, thumbs down.
- Write a paragraph in a planner, research log or journal.

Step 2: Plan of Action

This is a 2-fold step; students develop the questions they need to answer for the project and begin to develop strategies for answering the question or problem. The ultimate goal is for students to become capable of determining the questions necessary to institute the research to answer the problem. Too often librarians and teachers map out the strategies and information necessary for each problem. The goal of the Plan of Action is for students to identify the information needed and where they can go to find that information.

The teacher or librarian for the primary students usually does the identifying and selecting of the most appropriate resources. But by third grade students should learn through teaching and experience how to identify the possible resources and how to evaluate them for appropriateness. As a part of this experience students should learn to differentiate between primary and secondary sources. Students should also understand that the Internet is not the place to start the search. Basic print encyclopedias should provide general background knowledge. To add to the background knowledge, students can then use almanacs, databases (online or CD) and the Internet.

This is where the most instruction of new skills takes place; how to use an index, how to use an online database, etc.

- Fill out assignment planner part 2 (figure 5-1).
- Brainstorm—students share or list as many topics as possible with no thought as to accuracy or relevancy at this point.
- Create possible questions.
- Broaden or narrow a topic.
- Develop schema (relate to prior knowledge).
- Use a KWL organizer (Know/Want to Know/Learned).
- Quickwrite/Talk/Draw/Web—A strategy of writing that allows students to realize what they already know. Students write without stopping for one to three minutes, listing anything that comes to mind about the topic without worrying about spelling, punctuation or grammar. The same strategy can be used by drawing or talking.
- Create a web—can be electronic such as Kidspiration™.
- Cluster/Categorize—Grouping ideas to organize or gain focus for research.
- Use a Search Strategy Bookmark and an Information Checklist of Sources (figure 5-3). Fold the page in half lengthwise for a handy reference bookmark that keeps a list of questions students need to continually ask themselves as they move through the process and a list of readily available resources.
- For younger students provide a generic pathfinder page (figure 5-4). Write in learning logs or journals (Buehl, 2005)—Students learn to keep an on going account of their research process. It should start with the questions or information needed and end with the self-evaluation of the entire process.

- Do interviews—A source of primary material. Students learn how to conduct an interview and how to record the information gathered.

Step 3: Doing the Job

Once students have an idea of the questions to be answered and where to start locating the information, they begin to collect and organize that information. At the same time they need to keep looking back at the assignment to be sure they are following the parameters and the timeline.

These skills may need to be introduced or reviewed before starting a project. During the collaborative planning process, assess the student's knowledge of the particular skill needed. The actual teaching/reviewing then becomes a part of step 2.

- Fill out assignment planner part 3 (figure 5-1).
- Develop search strategies, i.e. key word, Boolean.
- Check resources for appropriateness and accessibility.
- Use information retrieval skills, i.e. encyclopedia and periodical indexes, card catalog subject headings, thesauruses, dictionaries.
- Learn about other resources outside of the school library media center, i.e. public libraries, museums, the Internet.
- Write letters, e-mails to experts.
- Telephone experts.
- Know how to skim and scan when reading materials and when each can be used to an advantage.
- Collect resources, read, reread, summarize, and paraphrase.
- Take notes and organize.
- Librarian or aide writes down the answers on a whiteboard as students identify needed information while resource is being read aloud.
- Students from upper grades or volunteer adults can buddy up to read and help collect information.
- Use "Trash 'n Treasure" (Jansen, 1996). Provide for each student a paragraph or short article on the selected topic. Have students search the text for answers to predetermined questions. The words or short phrases that answer the questions are "treasure" and are circled. Other words are "trash" and have a line drawn through them. "Treasures" are used to organize and synthesize information.
- Use note cards.
- Use data charts or a matrix for note-taking. Fold a legal size paper into 16 squares creating a matrix. Sources used for research are recorded down the left side and the questions to be answered across the top. Students then fill in the intersecting squares with the facts. Eliminates copying because only a few words fit each square. For emerging researchers this can be done as a group activity. Older students may use the bottom row of boxes to summarize the information used for each specific question.

- "ABC LOU" for Note-taking—Each letter stands for a different note-taking strategy (GILLS, 2003)
- (A) Abbreviations
- (B) Bullets
- (C) Caveman Language (use short phrases)
- (L) Lists
- (O) One word for several (paraphrase)
- (U) Use your own words, cite your sources
- Use pocket folder outline (figure 5-5).
- Use file folder outline (figure 5-6).
- Create note strips by using recycled paper to cut and number strips for reference. One or two related sentences are written on each strip. The page number from the source is noted on the strip. When data collection is finished, strips are divided into categories that answer the problem. These categories become paragraphs in the final paper.
- Group facts with codes or colors. This strategy is particularly useful with whole class instruction at the primary level. After reading an easy non-fiction book, students relate facts and the LMS or teacher writes them on chart paper. Statements that fit together are given a symbol (#, *, etc.) or a dot of color. Statements are then organized by code or color into groups. Students may then arrange the various statements within a code into any order that makes sense to the reader. Once mastered this can be done individually.
- Use hierarchies that allow students to make associations among pieces of information and relate them to concepts they already know. Information can be organized into levels, i.e. super or sub-ordinates.
- Write an outline that may be computer generated.

Step 4: Product Evaluation

In this step students take all the data and create the final product. Throughout the whole process the teacher and the librarian must take care that there is student-produced documentation for each step. Collecting the notes, photocopies of print materials used with the important parts highlighted ("Trash 'n Treasure"), outlines, drafts, etc. all help slow down the act of plagiarism.

- Fill out assignment planner part 4 (figure 5-1).
- Review—Refer back to steps 1 and 2 to be sure that the assignment parameters have been met and that selected strategies have been used.
- Obtain teacher and/or family feedback.
- Ask peers to review work.
- Do a self-reflection piece.
- Review the questions—are all elements of the assignment answered?
- Review findings—is there enough appropriate material to answer the questions or are there holes?
- Use a research log/journal—useful to keep track of the various steps of the process and to keep record of the various sites and resources used.
- Refine presentation options.

- Develop presentation/project skills.
- Create written products, emphasizing writing process skills—RAFT (Role/Audience/Format/Topic) (Buehl, 2005). Students determine the role of the writer, who the audience will be, the format of the writing and the topic to be addressed. For example, the student might do a writing project where the role is a newspaper reporter. The audience would be the readers of the 1870s. The format of the written piece would be an obituary while the topic would be the qualities of General Custer. Or a trout could be writing to self in a diary about the effect of acid rain on the home lake.
- Develop a multimedia presentation.
- Create products that meet local communication objectives.
- Utilize "Alternatives to Written Reports" (figure 5-2).
- Practice presentations.
- Check for proper crediting of sources.

Step 5: Process Evaluation

In this step students look back at the just completed assignment to reflect on their work and their understanding of the research process. This is the step most often neglected and yet it is the most important if indeed students are to learn from the activity and apply it the next time they are confronted with a similar situation.

- Fill out assignment planner part 5 (figure 5-1).
- Assess the process.
- Reflect on notes and resources used.
- Reflect on the product/project.
- Pick out best parts to put in a portfolio.
- Use rubrics for each step to assess the product/process.
- Younger students fill out a reflection paper using smiling faces for each level of achievement.
- Brainstorm worst/best parts of the activity.
- Institute a class discussion (particularly for the younger students).

RESOURCES FOR APPLYING THE HANDY 5 AS A WHOLE PROGRAM

Once all the individual steps of the Handy 5 model have been introduced to the students the student workbook becomes a useful tool.

STUDENT HANDBOOK

Each student handbook includes a working page for each step of the Handy 5 or may include fewer pages, depending on the number of steps used for the particular lesson. The teacher may include further directions for a particular lesson, i.e., on the How Do I Get the Job Done page, include at least 3 sources. Students could use the back of the page if more room is needed. See figure 5-7 for examples. A black-line master can be found on the Toolkit CD in the Student–Teacher Handbook file.

TEACHER MODEL

The model is based on the information from the poster and can be enlarged to fit colored legal paper or cardstock, and used as another way to introduce the model. If the primary model has been used it would be beneficial to use the appropriate colors for the first, third, and fifth steps. Add the name of the steps and parameters to the front of the hand. The hands are then cut out and bound on the "wrist end" to form a book. The model could also be used as a review strategy if the step name is placed on the front of the hand and the parameters on the back. The step could be displayed and used to generate discussion as to what happens during this part of the process. Students can then check themselves when the back of the hand is revealed. A black-line master can be found on the Toolkit CD in the Student–Teacher Handbook file.

LIBRARY PASS

Using a double-sided bookmark as a library pass is another way to keep the Handy 5 steps in front of the students all of the time and can demonstrate real-life application. Once the book-mark has been copied, fold it in half so the "library pass" is on one side and the steps are on the other side. Students can use the steps to remind them of their purpose for going to the library. Teachers can use it to send notes to the LMS as to the purpose of the student's visit to the library. Not all steps of the Handy 5 may be needed for each visit. See figure 5-8 for an example; a black-line master is located on the Toolkit CD in the Bookmark-Passes file.

SUMMARY

Teachers and LMSs have a large repertoire of teaching strategies at hand that are used on a daily basis. By thinking how best they support the various steps of the Handy 5 Model, it becomes obvious that learning many new skills is not necessary. Just be aware of which strategies work best with which steps. By using literature and other well-known strategies, integrating the model into the daily life of the classroom becomes much easier.

REFERENCES

Brown, Marc. *Arthur's Thanksgiving*. Boston: Little Brown & Company, 1983.

Buehl, Doug. *Classroom Strategies for Interactive Learning*. Newark, DE: International Reading Association, 2005.

Guide to Integrated Information Literacy Skills. Lincoln, NB: Lincoln Public Schools Library Media Services, 2003.

Jansen, Barbara A. "Reading for Information: The Trash 'n Treasure Method of Teaching Notetaking." *School Library Media Activities Monthly*. Vol. XII, No. 6, February 1996, 29-32.

Sharmat, Marjorie. *Nate the Great and the Missing Key*. New York: Bantam Doubleday Dell Books, 1981.

Figure 5-1 Handy 5 Assignment Planner

1 Name: _____ Room: _____

Fill out Assignment Planner steps #1-4 before you begin to work on your assignment. Fill out #5 before you turn your assignment in to your teacher.

What information do I need in order to do this?

2

What are the possible resources to find this information?

__Almanac   __Atlas
__Card catalog/OPAC
__Community resources (people/places)
__Dictionary   __Encyclopedia
__Electronic media   __CD-ROM
__Indexes   __Internet
__Library Media Center
__Public library   __Interview
__Non-print materials   __Magazines

Which ones are best for me to use?

Why?

3

Where will I find these resources?

Who can help me find what I need?

How will I record the information I find?

__take notes on cards
__take notes on paper
__take notes on a graphic organizer
__draw pictures
__other

How will I give credit for my resources?

__write title, author, page number on cards
__write title, author, page number on paper
__write title, author, page number on graphic organizer
__other

Figure 5-1 (continued) Handy 5 Assignment Planner

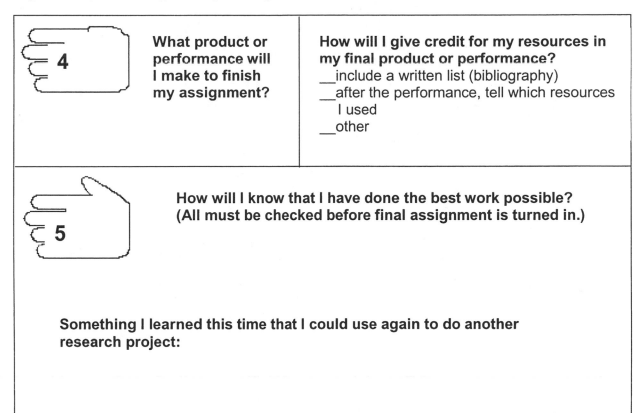

4 **What product or performance will I make to finish my assignment?**

How will I give credit for my resources in my final product or performance?
__include a written list (bibliography)
__after the performance, tell which resources I used
__other

5

How will I know that I have done the best work possible? (All must be checked before final assignment is turned in.)

Something I learned this time that I could use again to do another research project:

Figure 5-2 Alternatives to Written Reports

Alternatives to Written Reports

There are many lists of alternatives to written reports in the general school library literature. Here are just a few examples to jog the memory.

ART

Animation
Banners
Baseball cards
Book jackets
Bulletin board
Dioramas
Flannel boards
Flipbooks
Labeled diagram
Make a book
Masks
Project cubes
Quilts
Scrapbooks
Wall hangings

MOVEMENT

Charades
Choral reading
Cooking
Creative drama
Dancing
Finger plays
Puppet performances
Reader's theater
Role-playing

WRITING

ABC books
Brochures
Bumper stickers
Character sketches
First-person stories
Greeting cards
Memory books
Newspaper articles
Position papers
Radio scripts
Storytelling
Travelogues

ORAL

Audiotapes
Debates
Dialogues
Panel discussion

TECHNOLOGY SPECIFIC

Charts
Computer animation
Computer graphics
Databases
Digital photographs
Digital video
Electronic slideshows
Multimedia presentations
Word-processing documents

Figure 5-3 Information Sources/Strategy Bookmark

Library Media Center Information Sources	**Search Strategy Bookmark**
	Pre-Plan Your Search Strategies

Library Media Center Information Sources

- ☐ Library Media Center
- ☐ Library Media Specialist & Staff
- ☐ Atlas
- ☐ Almanac
- ☐ Dictionary
- ☐ Print Encyclopedia
- ☐ Indexes
- ☐ Nonfiction Collection
- ☐ Magazines/Newspapers
- ☐ On-line catalog
- ☐ Electronic media
- ☐ CD-ROM
- ☐ Internet
- ☐ Online databases
- ☐ Online Encyclopedia
- ☐ Video/DVD
- ☐ Community People & Organizations
- ☐ Other libraries, Public, University
- ☐ Other

Permission granted by Lincoln Public Schools Library Media Services to use this material.

Search Strategy Bookmark

Pre-Plan Your Search Strategies

Things to think about:

Choose your topic:

_____

What do I want to know?

Is my topic too narrow or too broad?

What do I think I already know?

What questions do I need to ask?

What is my central search question?

What are key words? (Synonyms, related terms, various spellings, proper names, plurals.)

What might my completed project look like?

Who will be my audience?

Do I need to change my topic?

What resources are available? (See reverse side)

Figure 5-4 Pathfinder

A PATHFINDER FOR

Nonfiction Book Titles

Call Number

1.
2.
3.
4.

Periodicals

1. _____
2. _____
3. _____
4. _____

Videocassette/Filmstrips

Titles   Call Number

1.
2.

Reference Books/Encyclopedia

Titles   Call Number

1.
2.
3.

Informational CD-ROMS

Titles   Call Number

1.
2.

Internet Sites

1.
2.

Student Name _____   Room # _____

Figure 5-5 Creating a Pocket Folder

Instructions for Creating a Pocket Folder Outline

Materials
2 sheets of 8-1/2" x 11" paper (or 11" x 14")
stapler or tape

1. Fold one sheet of paper 3-1/2" from the bottom. Fold the first piece 5" from the bottom. (For younger students use the legal size and fold 1 sheet 4" and the second sheet 6" from the bottom. This gives more writing space.)

2. Insert the second sheet of paper inside the first sheet. Fasten the 2 sheets together by stapling or taping along the edges, creating 4 pockets.

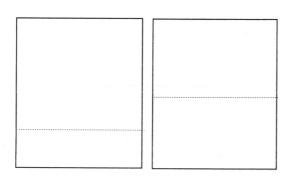

3. Use the pockets by having the student write the research question on the top of each pocket. Notes can be stored in the pocket behind the question.

4. A second way the pockets can be used (using the 11" x 14" paper) is to have students write the information on the front of each pocket and in what way it relates to the question.

Great Horned Owl
What does it eat?
What does it look like?
Where does it live?

Great Horned Owl
What does it eat?
What does it look like?
Where does it live? In many areas of the U.S. it likes barns and rural areas.

Permission granted by Lincoln Public Schools Library Media Services to use this material.

Figure 5-6 File Folder Outline

File Folder Outline
Materials
File folder for each student
Index cards or tag board or paper to make pockets

Front of file folder

Students write a research question on each index card. Cards are taped or stapled to the file folder to create pockets. As students write notes they are stuck in the pocket relating to the question. This helps students organize their notes before writing.

Have students write the assignment and/or timeline on an 8-1/2" x 11" sheet of paper. They can decorate the rest of the folder to illustrate the project if desired. Student name can be written on the file tab.

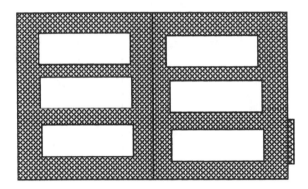

Staple a piece of paper on the back of the file folder where students can record resource information.

The file folder can also be used to store additional papers, etc. inside as various steps are finished.

Back of file folder

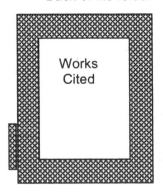

Works Cited

Permission granted by Lincoln Public Schools Library Media Services to use this material.

Figure 5-7 Student Handbook (*Toolkit CD-Student-Teacher Handbook*)

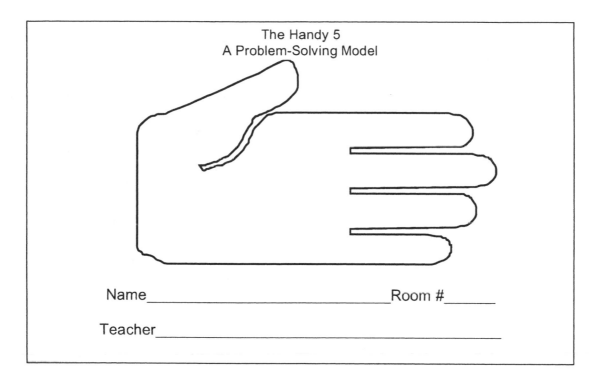

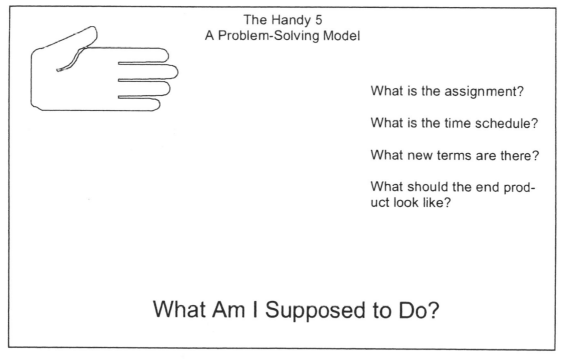

Figure 5-7 (continued) Student Handbook

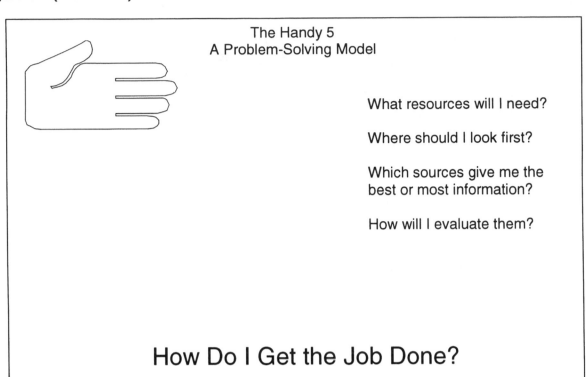

The Handy 5
A Problem-Solving Model

What resources will I need?

Where should I look first?

Which sources give me the best or most information?

How will I evaluate them?

How Do I Get the Job Done?

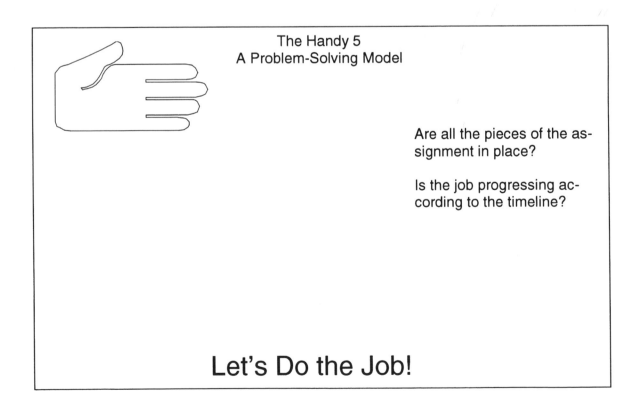

The Handy 5
A Problem-Solving Model

Are all the pieces of the assignment in place?

Is the job progressing according to the timeline?

Let's Do the Job!

Figure 5-7 (continued) Student Handbook

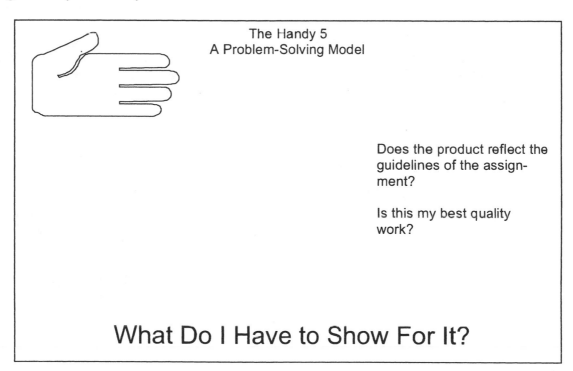

The Handy 5
A Problem-Solving Model

Does the product reflect the guidelines of the assignment?

Is this my best quality work?

What Do I Have to Show For It?

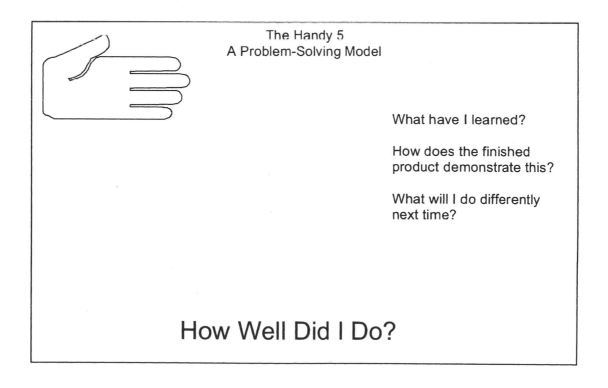

The Handy 5
A Problem-Solving Model

What have I learned?

How does the finished product demonstrate this?

What will I do differently next time?

How Well Did I Do?

Figure 5-8 Library Pass Bookmark (*Toolkit CD*-Bookmark–Passes)

Library Pass

FOLLOW THE HANDY 5
PROBLEM-SOLVING MODEL
AND FILL IN THE STEPS TO
COMPLETE YOUR JOB OR
ASSIGNMENT IN THE
LIBRARY.

TEACHER _____

_____

DATE _____

TIME _____

Librarian Information

Time In_____

Time Out _____

Developed by JK Stover 2005

The Handy 5

1. What am I supposed to do?

2. How do I get the job done?

3. Let's do the job!

4. What do I have to show for it?

5. How well did I do?

6

The Model as a Collaborative Planning Tool

Description of Collaborative Planning

Use of the Handy 5 in Collaborative Planning

Explanation of the Handy 5 Planning Sheet

A Lesson Plan Example for a Fifth Grade Unit

Designing Rubrics for the Handy 5

Criteria and Rubrics for Each Step of a Unit Plan

Summary

DESCRIPTION OF COLLABORATIVE PLANNING

Collaboration has been defined as "a working relationship over a relatively long period of time requiring shared goals, derived during the partnership. Roles are carefully defined, and more comprehensive planning is required" (Grover 1996, 2). Collaborative, integrated introduction has not flourished because few educators reflect on the planning process and therefore fail to understand how it occurs. If the LMS and teachers are to become true teaching partners, both must recognize the practice and methods of planning used by themselves and their partners. Curriculum planning, delivery of instruction in the content area, and teaching information literacy skills need to be integrated with learning activities that are shared in a full partnership between the LMS and the teacher.

Collaboration plays an essential role in student learning. Beneficial results of collaboration have been enumerated (Grover), and include the following:

- Collaboration "ignites" creativity among teachers, and the "creative fire" spreads to learners.
- Modeling collaboration results in more collaboration among faculty in the school.
- Modeling collaboration influences students, teachers, and parents, who learn to share ideas,
- Teachers, principals, and librarians communicate more frequently.

In this process of collaborative planning, the LMS becomes a leader in curriculum planning. The LMS, as a regular member of the school faculty, has firsthand knowledge of the school setting, its curriculum policies, administrative expectations, and teachers' personalities. The LMS also has expert knowledge of the curriculum for the building and the available resources. When knowledge of the planning process is added to this body of expertise, the LMS can respond to each request for help in planning, and can extend that request by making suggestions that can improve and enhance the process. Also, in a leadership role, the LMS can initiate joint planning and serve as a model for collaborative planning.

A district's adopted curriculum material, instructor guides, and materials collected by the teacher can influence the type and amount of planning done (Wolcott 2005). Also, the learners, the environment in which the learning takes place, and the planning process used by staff are important. If the LMS and teachers understand the implications these issues can have on planning, they can then be of help to one another in developing and using a planning process. Successful planning sessions are those in which all of these issues have been thoroughly considered, alternatives examined before choices are made, and planners can justify the collaborative, integrated decisions.

Together, all individuals in the planning process must reflect on teaching and learning. Knowing that planning is a mental activity that is often not consciously thought about, the LMS can help the teacher reflect on the common grounds they share. These experiences can serve as a springboard for discussion about teaching, student learning, and the impact it can have on integrated planning.

Information Power: Building Partnerships for Learning (AASL 1998) supports the need for collaboration in Learning and Teaching Principles of School Library Media Programs. Specifically principle 3 states: The library media program models and promotes collaborative planning curriculum development (pp. 63-64). In examining goals to assist the LMS in meeting this principle, it is suggested that the basis for planning is to use the information literacy standards for student learning. Regular communication to design integrated instruction and to deliver these standards is necessary. Once the instruction and method of delivery are determined, then a student's achievement must be assessed.

USE OF THE HANDY 5 IN COLLABORATIVE PLANNING

The Handy 5 was designed to facilitate student learning in all grade levels and subject areas as well as to serve as a collaborative planning framework for integrated instruction. In fact, the research indicated that the model is an effective tool for fostering collaboration among LMS and teachers. The findings further add that the Handy 5:

- Facilitates a transformation of the LMS role to that of a collaborating teacher of information skills.
- Helps structure planning with teachers.
- Results in a more effective use of time.
- Improves communication by establishing a common language.

Overall, the use of the model provides a step-by-step framework for planning, building, and delivering a unit.

Figure 6-1 Steps of the Handy 5

1. Assignment
2. Plan of Action
3. Doing the Job
4. Product Evaluation
5. Process Evaluation

The principle of collaboration advocated in *Information Power: Building Partnerships for Learning* correlates with the Handy 5 by showing the information literacy skills as the hub that serves all grade levels and subject areas: the pivotal, visual link between information literacy and content area standards. The model actually forms a framework that can be used by the LMS as a communication tool for working with teachers in collaborative planning. Even if one of the partners does not like to write everything down, or continues to make planning a mental activity, written notes must be used at some time. If the unit goes well, and learning occurs, this unit should be used again. If a successful unit is recorded at the time it is being planned and implemented, minimal time will be needed to plan for its use the next time.

A collaborative planning sheet has been developed by Kansas library media specialists specifically to use with the Handy 5. Examples of unit plans using this form can be found in Chapter 9. Figure 6-2 has had some explanation of the steps added to it.

Figure 6-2 Collaborative Planning Outline (*Toolkit CD*-Miscellaneous)

Collaborative Planning Outline

Standards Accomplished Addressed

Where does this assignment fit? What curriculum objectives will it fulfill?

1.	**Library Media Standards:**	*Indicate here which library media standards and curriculum content standards can be met through this unit. This will make alignment of the objectives easier, as well as provide*
2.	**Collaborative Content Standards:**	

Level: (grade or department)   **Teacher's Name:**

Title: (actual unit title) *Should be catchy and descriptive of the unit.*

Time to Be Completed: How many instructional periods are needed, how long are the periods?

One-Sentence Summary of the Assignment: What is the student to do? (Step 1) What will he have to show for it? (Step 4) *This will help planners understand the purpose of the lesson, who is involved, and what the final product will be.*

Finished Product Evaluation: What are the criteria and method by which the student will be graded? (Step 4)

- *This will let the students know in advance*
- *what he or she will be graded on.*

Plan of Action: What activities will be used to reach the assignment outcomes? What new information will need to be presented? (Step 2)

Library Media Specialist

a.   *LMS writes the strategies necessary*
b.   *to meet the lesson objectives here.*
c.
d.

Classroom Teacher

a.   *Classroom teacher writes the*
b.   *strategies necessary to meet the*
c.   *lesson objectives here.*
d.

Notes about Doing the Job: How is the unit developing; is the plan working? (Step 3)
 Observations about students, ideas for changes, pacing, etc., are noted here.

Process Evaluation: How well did it go; what should be done differently next time? Documentation for student achievement, i.e., % of students reaching benchmark. (Step 5)

 This is done at the end of the unit. Note changes in content, need for additional resources, etc.

Student Assessment Measures: Student product that assesses each step.

1. Assignment—
2. Plan of Action—   *The criteria assessing each step of the model*
3. Doing the Job—   *can be recorded here. This will help planning*
4. Product Evaluation—   *partners know what the end product will look*
5. Process Evaluation—   *like, as well as each of the necessary steps for*
                              getting there.

Materials/Resources: Include only special requirements.

Plan of Action: Individual Lesson

Objective: (For today's lesson. There can be as many or as few objectives as necessary to do a day's lesson)

Introduction: (Engaging students in the learning)

Activity 1: (Description of the way learning is to occur–may or may not be assessed at this time)

Activity 2: (Description of the way learning is to occur–may or may not be assessed at this time)

Assessment: (May be done at a later date)

Student Reflection: (How is this going to help me to do the assignment, what was new today, etc.)

Teacher Reflection: (How well did the lesson go?)

EXPLANATION OF THE HANDY 5 PLANNING SHEET

A box located at the top of the planning sheet provides a place to indicate which standards (LM and the collaborative content) can be met through the use of this particular unit. Even though it looks like there is room for only one standard for each area, the format may be adapted to record multiple standards as needed. On the other hand, don't list every standard this lesson might meet. Pick out only the key standards. Over time and experience the best lesson for specific standards will evolve until all standards can be met throughout the course of a year's instruction. The library media standards usually are based on the information literacy standards for student learning from *Information Power: Building Partnerships for Learning.* Content standards can be derived from national standards or in some adopted form depending on the state/school district requirements. These standards will help the LMS look for ways to integrate specific library skills into the classroom curriculum or the classroom teacher to integrate between content areas. The planners look at the unit and decide what the essential parts are and how they meet the different standards, enabling them to state a more precise student assignment.

The next part of the sheet provides a place to record the level, title, and completion time for this unit. The level should indicate the grade or department in which this unit will be used; the title should be catchy and descriptive of the unit; and the completion time is an estimate that may be changed as needed. It should be stated in the number of time periods needed, i.e. three 30-minute periods.

The assignment as a one-sentence summary is essential, and sometimes can be the most difficult part to formulate. It will help the planning partners understand what the purpose of the unit is, who is involved, and what the finished product will be. This part of the unit plan will have the planners focus on step 1 (assignment) and step 4 (product evaluation).

Once the objectives are finished and the assignment written, the planning partners identify the **finished product** for the project. Research on using the model has shown that assignment and finished product are intrinsically linked (see Chapter 8). Students should not be surprised by what is expected of them. Identifying and listing these criteria will help to develop the rubrics later. This part of the unit plan refers the planners to step 4 (product evaluation).

After the assignment and the finished product evaluation are determined, the **plan of action** is developed. The planning partners devise the strategies necessary to meet their unit objectives, i.e., what actual teaching activities are needed. This is also the place to assign responsibilities for the various unit elements. Some of the strategies might be taught by the individuals in their own classroom, while at other times, some of the strategies might be taught in a collaborative setting. The important thing is that the planning was done collaboratively. This part refers to step 2 (plan of action).

Notes about doing the job is filled in at the end of the daily lesson activity allowing the planning partners to see how that specific portion of the lesson went, and, if there is a need to add, to delete, or change any of the plan before the next day's lesson. It is also a place to write down student observations about the problem-solving process while it is happening. Doing this assures that the lesson will work smoothly the next time the unit is taught and helps provide for a thorough reflection during the unit evaluation.

Sometimes there is some confusion between the plan of action and notes about doing the job on the planning template. The plan of action details which specific tasks are needed and which task each partner will be responsible for in the overall unit plan. This will probably not be changed from one year to the next, unless major changes in the whole unit are made, based on process and product evaluation. Notes about Doing the Job could be new each time the lesson is presented as new students work though the process/project because new observations could occur based on the makeup and knowledge skills of the current class.

Process evaluation of the unit is undertaken when the students have finished the work. Corrections can be made when the unit is fresh—not the next year, when it is pulled out to be used again. Notes about additional resources and decisions made about the unit (i.e., what worked well, if students learned the intended outcomes) will help determine what, if any, changes need to be made before using the unit again. This is related to step 5 (process evaluation) of the Handy 5, where students have input into what worked well or needs to be changed.

There may not be any general expectations for each of the steps (if so, that may be indicated by the notation "NA"); however, this step in the planning helps the planning partners in determining what method of assessment will be used at each step. Decisions about what the students are going to be graded on become easier, as does the development of the rubrics, because there is a tangible assessment in mind.

One of the benefits of a plan and model such as this one is that it seems to fit the nonlinear way many teachers plan. Sometimes the finished product is already known, and the steps for getting there can be developed. Deciding what specific points the students are going to be accountable for might come next. The one-sentence summary statement might very well be the last piece of the picture. The main key is writing down as many of the parts of the overall plan as possible. Even if the team has to come back after teaching the first time through and write in what was done, the unit will be better and more solid the next time it is taught. The planners will have a better understanding of what are the most important components; the dialogue between the planners will improve and make true collaboration happen. Figure 6-3 demonstrates the order of the steps when used as a planning tool compared with when they are actually implemented.

Figure 6-3 The Order of the Handy 5 Steps: Changes from Planning to Implementation

Unit Planning	Unit Implementation
1. Assignment	1. Assignment
4. Product Evaluation	2. Plan of Action
2. Plan of Action	3. Doing the Job
3. Doing the Job	4. Product Evaluation
5. Process Evaluation	5. Process Evaluation

The second page of the Collaborative Planning Outline has evolved from experience. Practioners using the model kept asking for a way to track the daily plans necessary to carry out a unit plan. They kept inserting the daily plans in different places in the original template and it became too long and messy looking. The Planning Outline was envisioned to be a short 1-2 page document that gave the overall plan for the unit that could be pulled out each year and implemented with little or no change. It is intended that the Plan of Action: Individual Lesson would be added to the back of the Planning Outline as needed. In the example below refer to the sample lesson plan "Treasures of the Sea" figure 6-4.

Plan of Action: Individual Lesson

Each collaborative partner for a particular lesson will need a copy of this sheet with notes for their role.

Objective: (For today's lesson–there can be as many or as few objectives as necessary to do a day's lesson.)
To introduce/review the concept of "Trash 'n Treasures" as a way of locating key words to answer research questions.

Introduction: (Engaging students in the learning.)
Talk about going on a treasure hunt. Discuss how a map can help eliminate extraneous materials, can guide to specific clues. Locating materials to answer a question is a similar search for treasure clues.

Activity 1: (Description of the way learning is to occur–may or may not be assessed at this time.)
Model the activity on the overhead, circling words/phrases that answer questions; put a line through those words/phrases that do not answer the question.

Activity 2: (Description of the way learning is to occur–may or may not be assessed at this time.)
Individual work where each student has a photocopy article and locates trash 'n treasure.

Assessment: (May be done at a later date.)
Using transparency of student article, have students tell teacher which words to circle. Discuss any discrepancies.

Student Reflection: (How is this going to help me to do the assignment, what was new today, etc.)
Discuss how this method can be applied in other situations.

Teacher Reflection: (How well did the lesson go?)
After collecting individual student work, determine whether lesson was successful; if not, what needs to be done the next time the lesson is taught. Does any individual re-teaching need to be done before going on?

A FURTHER LOOK AT STANDARDS

As more and more school districts require their teachers to base their teaching on standards, one way for the LMS to get involved is to know those standards and how they align with the AASL literacy standards as outlined in *Information Power: Building Partnerships for Learning*.

Standards are important for several reasons. Three main ones are:
*   Standards serve to clarify expectations
*   Standards raise expectations
*   Standards provide a common set of expectations

Former Assistant Secretary of Education Diane Ravitch is commonly recognized as one of the chief architects of the modern standards movement. In her book *National Standards in American Education: A Citizen's Guide* (1995), Ravitch provides a common-sense rationale for standards. "Americans . . . expect strict standards to govern construction of buildings, bridges, highways, and tunnels; shoddy work would put lives at risk. They expect stringent standards to protect their drinking water, the food they eat, and the air they breathe. . . . Standards are created because they improve the activity of life" (pp. 8-9).

Ravitch asserts that just as standards improve the daily lives of Americans, so, too, will they improve the effectiveness of American education: "Standards can improve achievement by clearly defining what is to be taught and what kind of performance is expected" (p. 25).

How do the literacy standards align with the Handy 5? The writing committee offers the following as a way to meet them while using the problem-solving model.

Step 1: Assignment

1:1—Recognizes the need for information

Step 2: Plan of Action

1:2—Recognizes that accurate and comprehensive information is the basis for intelligent decision making
1:3—Formulates questions based on information needs
1:4—Identifies a variety of potential sources of information
1:5—Develops and uses successful strategies for learning information
2:4—Selects information appropriate to the problems or questions at hand
4:2—Designs, develops, and evaluates information products and solutions related to personal interests (also fits Steps 3 and 5)
6:2—Devises strategies for revising, improving, and updating work
7:1—Seeks information from diverse sources, context, disciplines, and cultures
8:2—Respects intellectual property rights (devises ways of citing sources)

Step 3: Doing the Job

2:1—Determines accuracy, relevance, and comprehensiveness
2:2—Distinguishes among fact, point of view, and opinion
2:3—Identifies inaccurate and misleading information
3:1—Organizes information for practical application
3:4—Produces and communicates information and ideas in appropriate formats

4:1—Seeks information related to various dimensions of personal well-being, such as career interests, community involvement, health matters, and recreational pursuits
5:2—Derives meaning from information presented creatively in a variety of formats
5:3—Develops creative products in a variety of formats
7:2—Respects the principle of equitable access to information
8:1—Respects the principles of intellectual freedom
9:3—Collaborates with others, both in person and through technologies, to identify information problems and to seek their solutions

Step 4: What Do I Have to Show for It?

3:2—Integrates new information into one's own knowledge
3:3—Applies information to critical thinking and problem solving
8:3—Uses information technology responsibly
9:1—Shares knowledge and information with others
9:2—Respects others' ideas and backgrounds and acknowledges their contributions
9:4—Collaborates with others, both in person and through technologies, to design, develop, and evaluate information products and solutions

Step 5: How Well Did I Do?

6:1—Assesses the quality of the process and products of personal information seeking

Figure 6-4 Treasures of the Sea Collaborative Planning Outline

Collaborative Planning Outline

Standards Accomplished in This Lesson
Where does this assignment fit? What curriculum objectives will it fulfill?
1. **Library Media Standards:** Standard I—The student who is information-literate accesses information efficiently and effectively.
2. **Collaborative Content Standards:** (Social Studies) Students will identify the living and nonliving resources of the ocean.

Level: (grade or department) 5th Grade Science   **Teacher's Name:** Mrs. Jones
Title: (actual unit title) Treasures of the Deep
Time to Be Completed: (how many instructional periods are needed, how long are the periods?) Eight 45-minute sessions

One Sentence Summary of the Assignment: What is the student to do? (Step 1) What will he have to show for it? (Step 4)

The student will research, with a partner, a product from the sea that is useful to man and prepare a museum exhibit with realia and facts.

Finished Product Evaluation: What are the criteria and methods by which the student will be graded? (Step 4)

- Completeness and quality of the graphic organizer
- Appropriateness of display items for the museum
- Completeness and quality of fact cards
- Cooperative skills

Plan of Action: What activities will be used to reach the program outcomes? What new information will need to be presented? (Step 2)

Library Media Specialist
a. Teach Trash/Treasure Note-Taking Model.
b. Help students locate resources, fill out data charts.
c. Set up museum with student help.

Classroom Teacher
a. Introduce concept of a museum and organize into cooperative groups.
b. Oversee locating materials and filling out data charts.
c. Coordinate with computer lab to help type fact cards.

Notes about Doing The Job: How is the unit developing; is the plan working? (Step 3)

It seems to be working well about midway through. Research is taking longer than expected. Some of the material is too difficult. Too many questions for students to handle in the amount of time allowed. Display went up well and looks attractive.

Process Evaluation: How well did it go, what should be done differently next time? Documentation for student achievement, i.e., % of students reaching benchmark. (Step 5)

The project went very well and met the objectives. The number of articles used needs to be decreased. The Internet articles were too difficult and had too many extraneous materials. Use only the magazine articles next time. Need more materials in the mineral and medicine sections.

Student Assessment Measures: kid product that assesses each step
1. Assignment—Completed assignment organizer (figure 6-5)
2. Plan of Action—Develop questions/graphic organizer (figure 6-6)
3. Let's Do the Job—-Fill out graphic organizer, data chart (figure 6-7)
4. Product Evaluation—Museum exhibit, fact cards (figures 6-8)
5. Process Evaluation—Student reflection of project (figure 6-9)

Materials/Resources:
URLs, pictures from *Ranger Rick*, data chart, graphic organizer, assignment planner

Figure 6-5 Treasures of the Sea: Assignment Planner

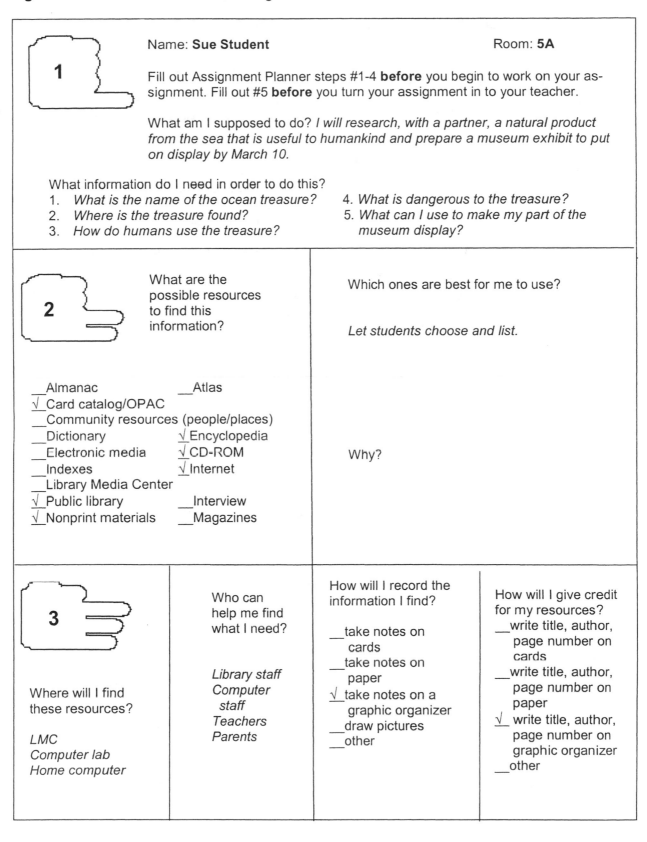

1

Name: **Sue Student**   Room: **5A**

Fill out Assignment Planner steps #1-4 **before** you begin to work on your assignment. Fill out #5 **before** you turn your assignment in to your teacher.

What am I supposed to do? *I will research, with a partner, a natural product from the sea that is useful to humankind and prepare a museum exhibit to put on display by March 10.*

What information do I need in order to do this?
1. *What is the name of the ocean treasure?*
2. *Where is the treasure found?*
3. *How do humans use the treasure?*
4. *What is dangerous to the treasure?*
5. *What can I use to make my part of the museum display?*

2

What are the possible resources to find this information?

Which ones are best for me to use?

Let students choose and list.

__Almanac   __Atlas
√ Card catalog/OPAC
__Community resources (people/places)
__Dictionary   √ Encyclopedia
__Electronic media   √ CD-ROM
__Indexes   √ Internet
__Library Media Center
√ Public library   __Interview
√ Nonprint materials   __Magazines

Why?

3

Where will I find these resources?

LMC
Computer lab
Home computer

Who can help me find what I need?

Library staff
Computer staff
Teachers
Parents

How will I record the information I find?

__take notes on cards
__take notes on paper
√ take notes on a graphic organizer
__draw pictures
__other

How will I give credit for my resources?
__write title, author, page number on cards
__write title, author, page number on paper
√ write title, author, page number on graphic organizer
__other

Figure 6-5 (continued) Treasures of the Sea: Assignment Planner

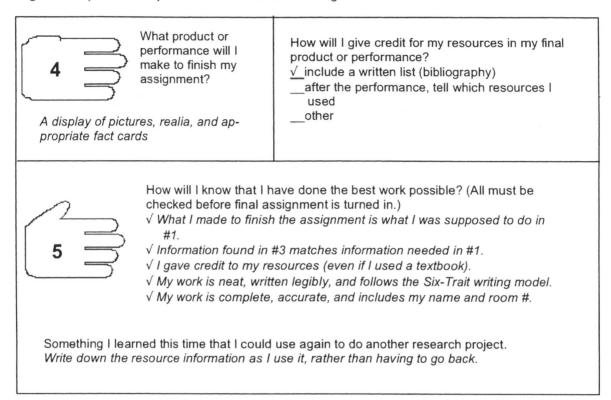

4

A display of pictures, realia, and appropriate fact cards

What product or performance will I make to finish my assignment?

How will I give credit for my resources in my final product or performance?
√ include a written list (bibliography)
__ after the performance, tell which resources I used
__ other

5

How will I know that I have done the best work possible? (All must be checked before final assignment is turned in.)
√ What I made to finish the assignment is what I was supposed to do in #1.
√ Information found in #3 matches information needed in #1.
√ I gave credit to my resources (even if I used a textbook).
√ My work is neat, written legibly, and follows the Six-Trait writing model.
√ My work is complete, accurate, and includes my name and room #.

Something I learned this time that I could use again to do another research project.
Write down the resource information as I use it, rather than having to go back.

Figure 6-6 Treasures of the Sea: Graphic Organizer

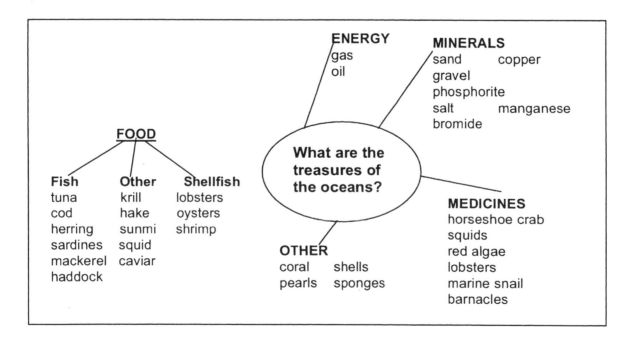

ENERGY
gas
oil

MINERALS
sand   copper
gravel
phosphorite
salt   manganese
bromide

FOOD

What are the treasures of the oceans?

Fish   **Other**   **Shellfish**
tuna   krill   lobsters
cod   hake   oysters
herring   sunmi   shrimp
sardines   squid
mackerel   caviar
haddock

OTHER
coral   shells
pearls   sponges

MEDICINES
horseshoe crab
squids
red algae
lobsters
marine snail
barnacles

Figure 6-7 Treasures of the Sea: Data Chart (*Toolkit CD*-Miscellaneous)

Name/Topic	Question #1 What Is the classification and name of your ocean treasure?	Question #2 What are the various names of the species, if any	Question #3 What Is the location of the treasure?	Question #4 How does humankind use the treasure?	Question #5 What is dangerous to the treasure?	Question #6 What are other interesting facts?
Example: Living Food	Crustaceans, mollusks, fishes, etc.	List different names	Ocean, country, ocean layer		Man and how!	Anything else you think the public should know
Source #1 "Oceans" *World Book Ency.*, Vol. 14, pgs. 653-654	Fishes	Anchovy, cod, herring, mackerel, sardines, haddock	Coastal waters	Food	NA	200 million lbs. of fish caught each year.
Source #2 Robinson, W. Wright. *Incredible Facts About the Ocean*. Minneapolis, MN: Dillon Press, 1990	Fishes—pg. 33	Sardines, anchovies, tunas, sharks, rays, and herrings—pg. 34	NA	...Most important source of food—pg. 34	Over-fishing, pollution, natural changes in the ocean—pg. 39	Fish can be raised like wheat on fish farms—called aquaculture—pg. 38
Source #3 Internet	URL name & key notes	URL name & key notes	URL name & key notes	URL name & key notes	URL name & key notes	URL name & key notes
Source #4 *Ranger Rick* magazine	pg #	pg #	pg #	pg #	pg #	pg #
Source #5 Other NF book (write resource information)	pg #	pg #	pg #	pg #	pg #	pg #
Summary Statement	My ocean treasures are called fish.	There are many kinds of fish; anchovies, cod, haddock, etc.	Most of the fish are caught in coastal waters	Man uses fish mostly for food	Man is dangerous to fish through over-harvesting, pollution, etc.	
What do I need to make my part of the museum display?	Pictures of the different types of fishes; a can of tuna or sardines					

Figure 6-8 Treasures of the Sea: Fact Cards

**Type of Treasure:
Living—Food
Crustacean
Crabs**

Specie names: Blue Crab, Dungeness Crab, Fiddler Crab

How used by humans: For food

Enemies: Humans, by over-fishing

Location: Pacific Ocean on continental shelf, Chesapeake Bay on the Atlantic
Ocean, near the water's surface and beaches

Any other interesting facts: Crabs have five pairs of legs and are called
decapods. The front pinchers may be broken off
during a fight and will regrow.

**Type of Treasure:
Nonliving—Energy
Petroleum**

How used by humans: Heating oil, in automobiles, machinery

Location: Off the Gulf of Mexico, deepest part of the ocean

Problems: Oil is located deeply under the seabeds and is expensive to extract

Any other interesting facts: Oil is pumped from land beneath the ocean, not the ocean
itself.

Figure 6-9 Treasures of the Sea: Student Reflection

Answer the questions below as you think about the project you just finished. Be sure to use all of the Six-Trait writing elements that apply.

In doing the research to create the museum display, you looked at several types of resources for your information.

- Which resource gave you the best information? Why?

  The Robinson book gave the most useful information about the types of fish and where they lived. I liked the Internet articles because they gave a lot of information, but some of them were really hard to read and understand.

- Which resource gave you the least information? Why?

  The Ranger Rick Magazine. There was no information, just a picture.

The treasure of the sea that you researched is helpful to humankind in some way.

- What are some of the environmental issues concerning humankind's responsibility to ensure that these treasures will continue to be available?

  Humans must learn to raise fish faster than they harvest them. Humans must also learn that many types of pollution affect the ocean water, even if they don't live close to the water.

- What can you as a student do to solve one of the problems facing the treasure that you researched?

  I can learn about the water resources in my own community and how to prevent pollution to them, because eventually the rivers here will run into the oceans. Other types of pollution can cause acid rain, which will dump bad materials into the ocean also.

DESIGNING RUBRICS FOR THE HANDY 5

Rubrics are an indication of success in measuring student progress toward a learning goal. Rubrics have been developed for the steps of the Handy 5 (for review, refer back to chapter 2). The model uses a rubric with four levels and one of nonachievement. Level 4 is the highest.

A rating of NA indicates that the student has produced no evidence of attempting to address the assignment. There is no basis for evaluation.

A rating of 1 indicates *Awareness*, or knowledge of the process or product, as indicated by evidence that the teacher and LMS have gathered. For example, in step 1 (the Assignment), the student in some way demonstrates awareness of the assignment or problem.

Understanding, a rating of 2, indicates that the student has demonstrated, often verbally, a basic grasp of the project.

Demonstration, a rating of 3, results from evidence provided by behavior and/or example.

Rating 4, *Application,* suggests that the student has synthesized the knowledge and is able to use it again in another situation (Grover).

CRITERIA AND RUBRICS FOR EACH STEP OF A UNIT PLAN

Rubrics should be developed for each of the five steps of the model that are used in the particular unit. By using the planning sheet to determine the specific elements that students are to be graded on and the finished product for each step of the model, planning partners find it relatively easy to write rubrics based on the particular unit or lesson.

In order to be most effective, rubrics should:
* Be written in such a way that students can understand and identify them;
* Be handed out at the beginning of the lesson; and
* Encourage students to become responsible for their own learning.

Assessment criteria—the specific guidelines for which students are to be held responsible in each section of the project—will be jointly devised by the teacher and LMS. Even though criteria are jointly devised, they may be for specific content objectives. For example, some criteria might have to do with fifth-grade science as well as the LMS's information skills objectives. The earlier section of the unit plan that asks for the finished product grading criteria is usually very general and relates to the entire project—e.g., the number of pages; bibliography required; final project of rough-draft stage. By defining the specific criteria in each step of the process, students will know in advance how to judge for themselves when each part of the project is finished and if the required quality of that section is present. Students will also begin to recognize if they need to back up and look again at the preceding step. The criteria can be easily adapted to each specific unit; the rubrics, which are written more generally, can be transferred from unit to unit with little modification. Ultimately, students will be able to assist in developing the rubrics themselves.

The rubric examples in figures 6-10 through 6-14 would complete the new lesson plan.

Figure 6-10 Treasures of the Sea: Rubric Assignment

ASSIGNMENT

Assessment Criteria
- Complete sections #1-4 of the assignment planner
- List the 4 parts of the assignment.
- Write the 5 questions to be answered by the project.

Rubrics
4—Demonstrates a thorough, complete understanding of the assignment by doing all the criteria correctly
3—Demonstrates a substantial understanding of the assignment by answering most of the criteria correctly
2—Demonstrates a partial/incomplete understanding of the assignment by answering some of the criteria correctly
1—Demonstrates a misunderstanding/serious misconception of the assignment by answering few of the criteria correctly
NA—Nothing available

Figure 6-11 Treasures of the Sea: Rubric Plan of Action

PLAN OF ACTION

Assessment Criteria
- Resource list in assignment planner has been marked with appropriate choices
- Graphic organizer is some type of central idea web
- Graphic organizer has correct topics and sea treasures listed

Rubrics
4—Uses the strategies provided in a highly effective manner by completing all the criteria correctly
3—Uses the strategies provided in an effective manner by completing most of the criteria correctly
2—Uses the strategies provided in a moderately effective manner by completing some of the criteria correctly
1—Uses the strategies provided in an ineffective manner by completing few of the criteria correctly
NA—Nothing available

Figure 6-12 Treasures of the Sea Rubric; Let's Do the Job

LET'S DO THE JOB

Assessment Criteria
- Appropriate resources are chosen
- Uses the "Trash 'N Treasure" Note-Taking Model on at least one resource
- Gives credit to sources using proper citation form
- Writes a summary statement for each question on the data chart

Rubrics
4—Is highly effective in implementing the plan of action by completing all the criteria correctly
3—Is effective in implementing the plan of action by completing most of the criteria correctly
2—Is moderately effective in implementing the plan of action by completing some of the criteria correctly
1—Is ineffective in implementing the plan of action by completing few of the criteria correctly
NA—Nothing available

Figure 6-13 Treasures of the Sea Rubric: Product Evaluation

PRODUCT EVALUATION

Assessment Criteria
- Data Chart is completed correctly
- Museum Display is neat and attractive
- Realia are appropriate to category
- Fact Cards are legible and accurate
- All working papers and display pieces are turned in on time
- Student contributes share of the project work in an appropriate way

Rubrics
4—Product reflects the student's thorough/complete understanding of the assignment by completing all of the criteria correctly
3—Product reflects the student's substantial understanding of the assignment by completing most of the criteria correctly
2—Product reflects the student's partial/incomplete understanding of the assignment by completing some of the criteria correctly
1—Product reflects the student's misunderstanding/serious misconception of the problem by completing few of the elements correctly
NA—Nothing available

Figure 6-14 Treasures of the Sea Rubric: Process Evaluation

PROCESS EVALUATION

Assessment Criteria
- Complete section #5 of the Assignment Planner
- Write a reflection in science journal about this project, following teacher's guidelines on expected writing standards

Rubrics

4—Is highly effective in evaluating the problem-solving process as indicated by answers in #5; the thoughtfulness of the answers and the quality of the writing in the reflection paper

3—Is effective in evaluating the problem-solving process as indicated by answers in #5; the thoughtfulness of the answers and the quality of the writing in the reflection paper

2— Is moderately effective in evaluating the problem-solving process as indicated by answers in #5; the thoughtfulness of the answers and the quality of the writing in the reflection paper

1— Is ineffective in evaluating the problem-solving process as indicated by answers in #5; the thoughtfulness of the answers and the quality of the writing in the reflection paper

NA—Nothing available

ADDITIONAL TOOLS

SCORING SHEET

A scoring sheet will be helpful for all members of the planning team to use. Team members can record their scores on the sheet, or each person can use an individual sheet. Figure 6-15 is one such example, completed for a student in the "Treasures of the Sea" unit.

There is a direct path from the form used in planning to presenting the lesson in "kid language," which has been explained in chapter 3. The parameters that help students understand each step of the model are also useful for the planners to use in developing lessons. A sample scoring sheet is found in figure 6-15.

Figure 6-15 Treasures of the Sea: Scoring Chart (*Toolkit CD*-Miscellaneous)

SUMMARY

In addition to being a problem-solving model, the Handy 5 is an excellent planning tool. It can be used to improve collaboration between classroom teachers and the LMS because it will help all members of the planning group speak a common language. The model will help planners make better use of their time, because once units are planned and implemented, the forms can be used again and again, thus allowing planning time to be used to create new units of study.

The Handy 5 also provides a system of record keeping. It reminds members of their specific responsibilities while the unit is being taught. It provides a place to write notes for changes the next time the unit is used. Some record should be made so that when the unit is used again, all the necessary information is available. The planning time can them be devoted to planning a new unit of study.

The model can be adapted to many different learning styles and theories. While the Handy 5 has been designed to be used most effectively in a K-12 setting, if it is not being used this broadly it can still work at a building level, or even by the individual LMS working in collaboration with interested classroom teachers.

REFERENCES

American Association of School Librarians and Association for Educational Communications and Technology. *Information Power: Building Partnerships for Learning.* Chicago: American Library Association, 1998.

Grover, Robert. *Collaboration.* Chicago: American Association of School Librarians, 1996.

Ravitch, Diane. *National Standards in American Education: A Citizen's Guide.* Washington, DC: Brookings Institution Press, 1995.

Wolcott, Linda Lachance. "Understanding How Teachers Plan: Strategies for Successful Instructional Partnerships." ALA/SLMR ©1999.
http://www.ala.org/ala/aasl/aaslpubsandjournals/slmrb/editorschoiceb/infopower/selectwolcott.htm (accessed 18 November 2005).

PART TWO

Why the Model
Is Important

7

Trends in Education Today: Professional Learning Communities

The Changing Role of the Library Media Specialist

General Trends

Professional Learning Communities

The Handy 5 as an Assessment Technique

Brain Research

THE CHANGING ROLE OF THE LIBRARY MEDIA SPECIALIST

No Child Left Behind (NCLB) has changed the teaching and learning focus in many districts. Lower elementary educators discover their days are dominated by the teaching of reading and mathematics in effort to meet the proficiency levels required by federal legislation. No time exists for other areas such as social studies, science, and information literacy (and sometimes even recess) unless district leadership takes on the role of supporting integrated curriculum. More than ever, the role of the library media specialist (LMS) goes beyond building collections, providing Internet access, flexible scheduling, and "programming." The role of the LMS, as articulated in *Information Power for Learning* (1998) is still relevant today in emphasizing active participation in instruction through collaborative teaching and assessing learning. The LMS is engaged as an equal partner with teachers in the planning, implementing, and assessing of learning. Although this task may seem overwhelming, it is the same dilemma as faced by the person who asked, "How do you eat an elephant?" The solution to both is "One bite at a time!"

The many changes in education result in this grand challenge to LMSs. In this chapter we present an overview of these trends and show what these trends mean for LMSs wanting to focus on student learning and creating dynamic integrated teaching/learning environments.

GENERAL TRENDS

Prior to No Child Left Behind, school reform and school improvement efforts, focused on setting goals or targets, then improving student performance. Teaming was integral to this process. As the sophistication of school improvement progressed, so has the terminology. Now, the emphasis is on the power of professional learning communities (PLC) to involving the entire staff to support each student's learning. Richard DuFour describes the big ideas of a PLC as:

Big Idea #1:   Ensuring That Students Can Learn
Big Idea #2:   A Culture of Collaboration
Big Idea #3:   A Focus on Results

In Big Idea #1, the change is from a focus on teaching to a focus on learning. Through the creation of standards, we ask, what can students learn and how will we know? The major difference with learning communities and traditional schools is the challenge of responding when a student has difficulty learning. In a learning community, staff works together to develop strategies that help the struggling student. According to DuFour (2005), these responses are:

- *Timely.* The school quickly identifies students who need additional time and support.
- *Based on intervention rather than remediation.* The plan provides students with help as soon as they experience difficulty rather than relying on summer school, retention, and remedial courses.
- *Directive.* Instead of *inviting* students to seek additional help, the systemic plan *requires* students to devote extra time and receive additional assistance until they have mastered the necessary concepts.

The LMS as part of the professional learning community often has a relationship with a students that is atypical of teachers. She sees a student struggling and is aware of ways to tap into and support the student from a library media program perspective. This is especially true at the high school level where the opportunity exists for the LMS to develop a relationship with students and engage them in learning focused on their interests. Due to this unique relationship, the LMS becomes a powerful, contributing member of the PLC.

Another aspect of the special relationship the LMS has with students is socioeconomic status. The library media center serves as a great leveler in society. Ruby Payne, in *A Framework for Understanding Poverty* (2005), shares that students from generational or situational poverty operate by a separate set of rules. In a classroom, these students need to complete projects, or parent/family input is needed at school activities. The student has to juggle excuses for not completing an assignment lacking financial resources or for reasons that a parent or family member does not meet the teacher. In contrast, the library media center is neutral territory with accessible resources. And, the LMS teaches the student information-literacy skills that enable him to be a problem solver and lifelong learner. In short, the LMS stands on the front line in *inviting* students to seek extra assistance and to know how to approach them in a manner that does not cause a loss of face.

Big Idea #2 refers to a culture of collaboration, a very natural state for the effective LMS. In spite of school improvement efforts that stress teaming, many teachers work in isolation, especially at the high school level. This problem of isolation is further complicated for the LMS who finds the library media program is being used as a teacher's planning time. Most of the day becomes a 20-30 minute cycling of students in and out of the library media center. Many LMSs lament the loss of collaborative planning time and additionally report that often they only have time to check materials in and out. Providing instructional time for information literacy is limited. However, in a professional learning community, teachers and the LMS collaborate in a systematic process to analyze and improve student learning. The Handy 5, with its built-in framework for working with teachers, is an excellent coupling with a PLC. In chapter 8, *The Handy 5* research showed:

The research findings indicate that the model is an effective tool in fostering collaboration among LMSs and teachers. The model facilitates a transformation of the LMS's role to that of collaborating teacher of information skills. Use of the model is an efficient use of time because it structures planning with teachers and improves communication by using a common language.

Big Idea #3 focuses on results, which is another strong link with the Handy 5. DuFour reports that schools and teachers typically suffer from the DRIP syndrome—Data Rich/Information Poor. The results-oriented professional learning community not only welcomes data but also turns data into useful and relevant data (p. 40). Steps 1-3 of the Handy 5 model lead to reflecting in Steps 4 and 5 on the quality of the product and what workcd well or did not work well with the process. The LMS and teacher collaborators embrace data as a measure of progress and honestly confront the teaching and learning practices that help or hinder student success.

Figure 7-1 Alignment of Professional Learning Community and the Handy 5

Professional Learning Community		Handy 5
• Big Idea #1: Ensuring That Students Can Learn • Big Idea #2: A Culture of Collaboration • Big Idea #3: A Focus on Results	→	• Assignment • Plan of Action • Doing the Job • Product Evaluation • Process Evaluation

ASSESSMENT FOR LEARNING

School library media specialists are involved in daily assessments of many kinds: student helpers, volunteers, library clerks, books, computer programs, and other materials, student assessment through library classes and teacher/librarian-developed assessments for classes, programs, and services in all subject areas. *Assessment* is a global term for the many ways that we measure student learning and achievement. It can be as simple as a teacher's subjective judgment on how a child holds a pair of scissors or the outcome of a two-week research assignment. It is considered most trustworthy when it is authentic and occurs as a regular part of classroom instruction in meeting the needs of the student (Hill and Ruptic 1994).

The Learning and Teaching Principles of School Library Media Programs as described in *Information Power: Building Partnerships for Learning* (1998, p. 58) advocate learning as a fundamental goal of the school staff. In order to determine if learning is taking place, methods of assessment must be developed. Grover (1993) stressed that the ongoing assessment of student progress, meaningful evaluation of that progress, and the reporting of this progress in a manner which communicates effectively to school staff, students, and parents are critical to the teaching/learning process. McTighe and Ferrara (1998) add, "The primary purpose of classroom assessment is to inform teaching and improve learning. Without multiple, accurate, and reliable assessments it is difficult to know if students are 'hitting the target' or, for that matter, are even aware of what the learning 'target' is or where it is located" (North Central Association Commission on Schools, 1995).

McTighe and Ferrara state that *assessment, testing,* and *evaluation* are terms that are often used interchangeably but have different meanings. This is because the assessment movement in the United States is synonymous with the growth of testing, and in particular, standardized testing.

- *Assessment* refers to gathering and synthesizing information.
- *Testing* is one type of assessment, such as a "bubble" sheet test. Tests are usually in a paper-and-pencil format, have time limits, restrict access to other resources, and have a limited range of acceptable responses.
- *Evaluation* has to do with making a judgment... "regarding quality, value, or worth, based upon criteria" (McTighe and Ferrara).

In examining these definitions, the Handy 5 is an assessment tool because the structure of the model allows the gathering and synthesizing of information for use by LMS, teacher, student, and parents. Loertscher and Woolls (1999) describe the Handy 5 as one of two major assessment tools using rubrics to determine student performance to appear in the literature.

Many of these elements are incorporated into the design of the Handy 5. The LMS and teacher(s) use curriculum aligned with instruction and assessment to impact the grading system. Low-achieving students can be quickly identified through use of the model, and instruction can be modified since student processes, products, and performances are constantly assessed by rubrics and benchmarks. The structure of the model also helped students to learn higher order thinking skills because the rubrics are designed to promote levels of effort, completion, and quality.

In conclusion, teachers who implement strategies that appeal to several learning styles make it possible for students to expand their opportunities to learn. The Handy 5 enables the teachers and LMS to plan collaboratively the process for learning in such a way that the learning outcomes are clear. The model introduces a common language and steps for organizing learning activities. When students understand what they are expected to know, they are more responsible and produce the desired results. This model is a blueprint for action that can be used by LMSs and teachers for the benefit of students. Our research showed that students did indeed produce a better product and asked better questions when the Handy 5 was used.

COLLABORATION WITH THE COMMUNITY

Collaboration for the LMS goes beyond the school community and encompasses many partnerships. School staff says they can't do everything that is expected by them. Teachers are not social workers, judges, or police officers. Schools must work with the community; for example, involving public library in reading programs for preschoolers. Consequently, the entire community must evolve from one in which the school is isolated to one in which there is collaboration among the school, parents, and other public agencies and service organizations–e.g., public library, police department, fire department, public health agencies, and other service organizations. The school must be viewed as a segment of a community fabric, interwoven with public and private-sector agencies and service organizations, as figure 7-2 indicates.

Figure 7-2 The AASL Learning Community

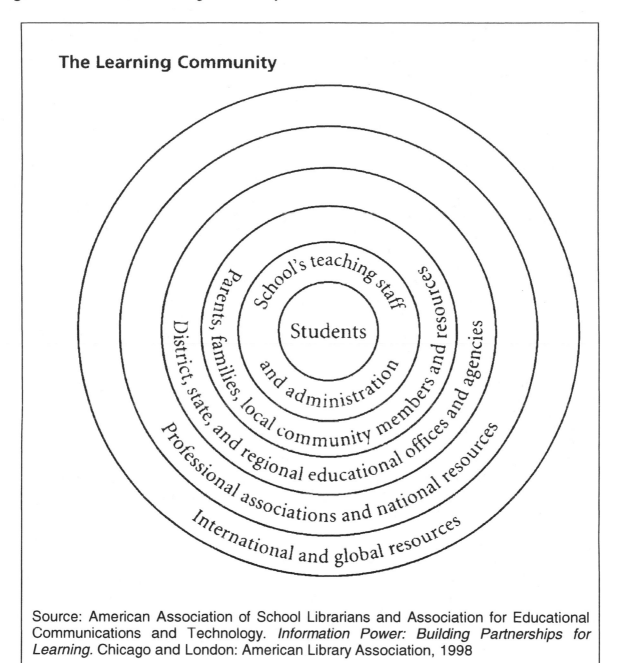

The Learning Community

Students

School's teaching staff and administration

Parents, families, local community members and resources

District, state, and regional educational offices and agencies

Professional associations and national resources

International and global resources

Source: American Association of School Librarians and Association for Educational Communications and Technology. *Information Power: Building Partnerships for Learning.* Chicago and London: American Library Association, 1998

In sum, everyone must work together to help each student become a productive member of society and a lifelong learner. This collaboration begins with birth, where hospitals notify schools of newborn children requiring special care—e.g., disabilities of various types. Federal and state monies are available through schools and other social service agencies for this care. There are programs such as Parents as Teachers, which prepare parents to recognize the developmental stages of their newborn children and to use this knowledge to stimulate their children's learning during these crucial formative years. This is the beginning of a community-wide partnership. The collaboration should continue and expand through the preschool and traditional school years to include various community groups and agencies, working with the school to assure children an education that will enable them to be productive members of the community and self-fulfilled members of society at large. The goal of this community partnership is to socialize children into our society for a productive role (a job), but it also includes preparing young people to appreciate the arts and cultural diversity so that they can enjoy a high quality of life. In addition, young people should be taught those values that result in participation in the democratic process. That socialization can be done effectively only when various elements of a community work together.

These ideas are not radical. Many business leaders think of their enterprises as "learning organizations" which foster lifelong learning among employees. Businesses have standards and look for ways to measure their outcomes (products or services) against those standards. For example, Tom Peters and Robert Waterman, in their work *In Search of Excellence: Lessons from America's Best-Run Companies* (1982), found that the most successful businesses continuously worked to provide excellence in their products or services. In *Thriving on Chaos: Handbook for a Management Revolution* (1987), Peters urges all organizations to try continuously to improve: "If it isn't broke, fix it anyway" (p. 3). Rapid change in our society today requires continuous review or assessment of our activities lest we become unproductive or unsuccessful.

Jim Collins in *Good to Great* (2001), states that good is the enemy of great. Even those LMSs who are doing a good job, as evidenced by their teachers', students', and principals' comments, need to continue to assess their involvement in the teaching of information skills and try to improve.

> Those who built the good-to-great companies were, to one degree or another, hedgehogs. They used their hedgehog nature to drive toward what we came to call a Hedgehog Concept for their companies. Those who led the comparison companies tended to be foxes, never gaining the clarifying advantage of a Hedgehog Concept, being instead scattered, diffused, and inconsistent. (p. 92)

In short, the LMS can use the teaching of information-literacy skills to be their hedgehog. Using a model such as the Handy 5 is a way to focus and clarify these skills so that students can apply them throughout their lives.

NATIONAL STANDARDS AND TESTS

To assure continuous productive change, most businesses develop a business plan. These plans serve as "road maps" of where they are and where they want to go. Many schools have developed similar "business plans" to deal with student learning, assessing where students are academically and where they need to go in order to be productive citizens and lifelong learners.

These "road maps" of where we've been, where we are, and where we want to go require standards and assessment; consequently, we are challenged to review our activities in terms of standards and formative and summative tests. This trend began in 1989 with the establishment of national education goals.

Information Power: Building Partnerships for Learning (1998) also emphasizes the teaching role of the LMS, extending it to one of partnership and leadership in the teaching of information skills as outlined in Information Literacy Standards. Collaboration with teachers is necessary to meet standards and assessments in which the LMS is an equal teaching/learning partner. As an equal partner, the LMS participates in planning a unit with the teacher, team teaching, evaluating the students' work, and assisting with students who are struggling to meet standards. The LMS is much more involved in all stages of teaching and learning, as shown in figure 7-3.

Figure 7-3 The *Information Power* Logo

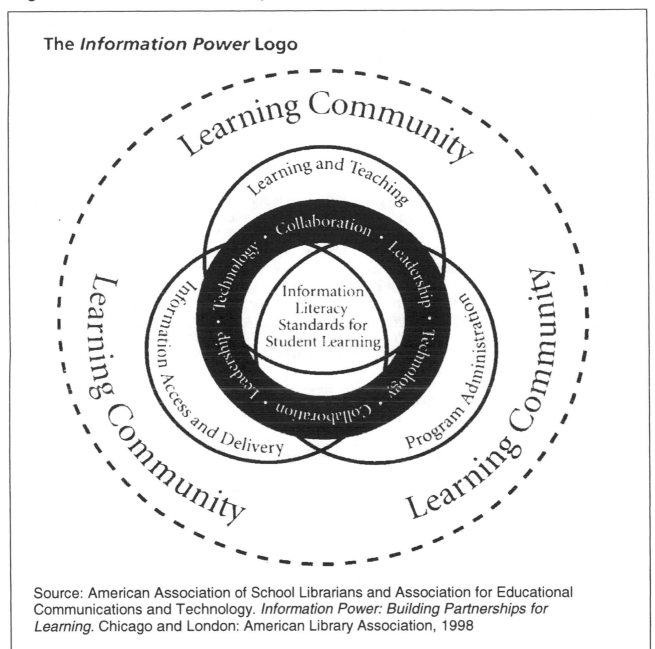

Source: American Association of School Librarians and Association for Educational Communications and Technology. *Information Power: Building Partnerships for Learning.* Chicago and London: American Library Association, 1998

POWER STANDARDS

The standards movement has undergone another transformation in language and impact with the power standards movement led by Douglas Reeves. Power standards must meet these three criteria:

- Endurance—longevity surpasses the length of state assessment.
- Leverage—associated with success in other standards.
- Essential for next level of instruction—critical need for this knowledge must be met to be promoted to the next grade level (*On Common Ground,* 2005, pp. 44-52).

The LMSs who use the Handy 5 collaborates with teachers. Both parties bring content standards to planning the assignment. An example of a power standard is Standard 6 from the Independent Learning Standards described in *Information Power: Building Partnerships for Learning*: "The student who is an independent learner is information literate and strives for excellence in information seeking and knowledge generation" (p. 29).

Information seeking and knowledge generation encompasses endurance, leverage, and essentialness, not only for the next level of instruction, but to be a lifelong learner.

THE HANDY 5 AS AN ASSESSMENT TECHNIQUE

In general, there is a saying that "whatever tasks are inspected gets respected." The research team who designed the Handy 5 took all of these issues into consideration when developing and implementing the model. Of special consideration was the role of the LMS in the assessment of student performance. Many of the LMSs who participated in the study saw themselves as resource people and, in some instances, co-designers of instruction. The role of coassessing the learning was foreign for most of the LMSs except as to how it related to the library media curriculum. After the study was completed, many of the participants shared that assessing student performance in the regular classroom enhanced the planning process with the teacher by use of a common language. The corollary that "Whatever is valuable enough to assess should be important to the curriculum" should be changed to "Whoever is valuable enough and has the skills to assess is important to the curriculum."

FORMATIVE AND SUMMATIVE EVALUATION EMBEDDED IN THE HANDY 5

There are two kinds of assessment: formative and summative. Formative assessments are ongoing and take place during the course of instruction. They are designed to help the teacher make adjustments in order to improve student performance. A teacher may ask students to make a list of all resources that the student has used in researching a project to date on a topic in order to ascertain the number, variety, and appropriateness of these sources in the information-gathering part of an assignment. Most classroom assessments are formative and usually involve the teacher's informal observations and questions.

Steps 1 to 4 of the Handy 5 model focus on formative assessments that guide the LMS and teacher in making sure the student is on target with the assignment, has a plan of action for choosing effective strategies, is able to implement the plan for completing the assignment, then actually generates a high-quality product.

Summative assessments are culminating assessments that provide a summary report on the proficiency attained at the conclusion of a course of study, a unit, a lesson, etc. For example, a teacher may ask that the student give an oral presentation of a book report. Other examples would be a test, a senior research project, a multimedia project, or a master's thesis. They generally require norm-referenced evaluations. Increasingly, portfolios are used for summative assessments. They can be criterion-referenced if the domains are well defined.

Step 5 of the Handy 5 evaluates Steps 1 to 4 of the model to determine if the problem-solving process used by the student was effective. In other words, did the student use every step of the model at least at benchmark or mastery level? If not, then the planning of the integrated unit needs to be reexamined in terms of problem areas related to the assignment, plan of action, doing the job, and finished product. If yes, then the LMSs, teacher, and student can be confident that the integrated unit was successfully completed.

BRAIN RESEARCH

Eric Jensen describes the science and practice of consistently involving nearly all students in *Tools for Engagement* (Jensen 2003). Engaging the learner is the responsibility of the LMS who must understand the relationship between engagement and knowledge of how the brain operates. These operations are how the brain's response system reacts to states. Some states are curiosity, happiness, frustration, anticipation, apathy, fear, and confusion. In fact, there are hundreds of states that come into play and are exhibited by students in the library media center.

The Handy 5, by the very nature of its five steps, allows for changing states by adding music. Rich Allen (Allen 2001) wrote:

> The fact that music can facilitate a state change in our mind/body makes it a potentially powerful tool for trainers. Not only can music, when it is used purposefully, reduce stress; it can enhance cognition, memory, perceptual-motor skills, and emotional intelligence. We also know that music can induce relaxation, creativity, self-discipline, and motivation.

As the LMS works with students using the Handy 5, Allen suggests some simple ways to use music to enrich the teaching environment. When students come into the library media center, play an up-tempo piece to energize the class. Often music from the 1960s or 1970s is a good choice because it is so familiar. These pieces are used as theme songs in many movies or television shows. Also, the golden oldies are often heard on radio stations, so the tunes can elicit an emotion. Some possible selections are:

- *Let's Get Ready to Rumble!* (Michael Buffer, from *Jock Jams*, 1995, Tommy Boy Music)
- Theme from *Rocky* (*Gonna Fly Now* by Bill Conti)

To change the state to where students are ready to learn, the LMS stops the music. Breathing– another way to change states–can be used. Jensen (p. 37) suggests the following:

> Use the release of breath to prompt an if-then scenario. You might ask the group to inhale slowly and then tell them, "If you are ready to begin, breathe out." Use the release of the breath for an additional release by saying, "If you're ready to learn (or feeling more relaxed), exhale slowly." Acknowledge their decision to move on with a simple "Good or Great!"

As the LMS moves into each step of the model, music can be played to introduce the step. Each time the student returns to the project during the next class session, the music for the step they are working on greets them. Some possible suggestions are:

Step 1: Assignment—What Am I Supposed to Do?
- *I Can See Clearly Now* (Johnny Nash)

Step 2: Plan of Action—How Do I Get the Job Done?
- *Takin' Care of Business* (Bachman Turner Overdrive)

Step 3: Doing the Job—Let's Do the Job!
- *Flight of the Bumblebee* (Nicolai Rimsky-Korsakov)
- *The Locomotion* (Little Eva)

An instrumental selection could be used as a musical pad while the students are busy working on doing the job. A possibility would be *Whistle While You Work* (Disney) or *Don't Worry, Be Happy* (Bobby McFerrin).

Step 4: Product Evaluation—How Well Did I Do?
- *Shout* (Isley Brothers)

Step 5: Process Evaluation—How Well Did I Do?
- *Walk Right In* (The Rooftop Singers)
- *Joy to the World* (Three Dog Night)

What did not work well and you would not do again?
- *Hit the Road Jack* (Ray Charles)

After Step 5 is completed for all students, songs such as *Celebration* (Kool and the Gang) and *1812 Overture* (Pytor Ilyich Tchaikovsky) can be played to signify the end of the assignment or project.

The LMS might want to establish guidelines for music selections that allow students to make choices based on the project. If astronomy is the topic of the assignment, all musical selections might be based on music with a star theme.

SUMMARY

More than a cosmetic change, a professional learning community requires a substantive change in school culture and the way that schools "do business." Using data to lead change includes standards as well as formative and summative assessments to make decisions. Also, changing school culture requires applying the newest instructional strategies based on brain research that engage the learner. The Handy 5 model presented in this book provides such a tool for LMSs and teachers to use to collaborate and implement culture changes in education that will prepare students for a productive future as lifelong learners.

REFERENCES

Allen, Rich. *TrainSmart: Perfect Training Every Time.* San Diego, CA: The Brain Store, 2001.

American Association of School Librarians and Association for Educational Communications and Technology. *Information Power: Building Partnerships for Learning.* Chicago and London: American Library Association, 1998.

Bridges, W. *Participants Guide: Pre-Work.* Mill Valley, CA: William Bridges & Associates, 1992.

Chalker, D. M. and R. M. Haynes. *World Class Schools: New Standards for Education.* Lancaster, PA: Technomic Publishing Co., 1994.

Collins, Jim. *Good to Great.* New York: HarperCollins, 2001.

Costa, A. L. and B. Kallick. *Assessment in the Learning Organization: Shifting the Paradigm.* Alexandria, VA: Association for Supervision and Curriculum Development, 1995.

A Design for Building Outcomes-Focused Curricula. May, Topeka, KS: Kansas State Board of Education, 1994.

DuFour, Richard, Robert Eaker, and Rebecca DuFour (editors). *On Common Ground.* Bloomington, IN: National Education Service, 2005.

Gardner, H. 1993. *Frames of Mind: The Theory of Multiple Intelligences.* Second paper ed. New York: Basic Books, 1983.

Grover, Robert. "A Proposed Model for Diagnosing Information Needs." *School Library Media Quarterly* 21, no. 2 (winter 1993): 95-100.

Hill, Bonnie Campbell and Cynthia A. Ruptic. *Practical Aspects of Authentic Assessment: Putting the Pieces Together.* Norwood, MA: Christopher-Gordon Publishers, Inc., 1994.

Jensen, Eric P. *Tools for Engagement: Managing Emotional States for Learner Success.* San Diego, CA: The Brain Store, 2003.

Loertscher, David V. and Blanche Woolls. *Information Literacy: A Review of the Research: A Guide for Practitioners and Researchers.* San Jose, CA: Hi Willow Research and Publishing, 1999.

McTighe, Jay and Steven Ferrara. *Assessing Learning in the Classroom (Student Assessment Series).* Washington, D C: National Education Association, 1998.

National Central Association Commission on Schools. *Writing and Evaluating Target Area Goals.* Tempe, AZ: North Central Association Commission on Schools, 1995.

National Education Report Goals Summary. Washington, D.C.: National Education Goals Panel. 1997.

Payne, Ruby. *A Framework for Understanding Poverty.* Highlands, TX: aha! Process, Inc. Rev. 2005.

Peters, Thomas J. *Thriving on Chaos: Handbook for a Management Revolution.* New York: Harper & Row, 1987.

Peters, Thomas J. and Robert H. Waterman. *In Search of Excellence: Lessons from America's Best-Run Companies.* New York: Harper & Row, 1982.

Process Module. Topeka, KS: Kansas State Board of Education, 1992.

Quality Performance Accreditation Manual. Topeka, KS: Kansas State Department of Education, 1997.

Senge, P. *The Fifth Discipline: The Art and Practice of the Learning Organization.* New York: Doubleday/Currency, 1990.

8

Using the Model: What Our Research Told Us

The Problem

Overview of the Study

Selecting Schools

Research Methods

Analysis of Data

Overview of Findings

Use of the Handy 5

Learning

Collaboration

Implications for Practice

Strengths of the Model

Needs Associated with Use of the Model

Summary

THE PROBLEM

In 1991, the Kansas State Department of Education began a statewide school improvement process when it adopted the Quality Performance Accreditation system. Unlike past accreditation methods, which had focused on such things as the number of books in libraries or the square footage of buildings, the new system accredits schools based on student performance; that is, a school's quality is judged by its students' academic performance and their continual academic improvement. Furthermore, this system requires all educators to collaborate in the design, implementation, and assessment of instruction.

Since 1993, the Kansas State Department of Education, in collaboration with educators throughout the state, has developed and adopted curriculum standards in the content areas of mathematics, communication, social studies, and science. LMSs in Kansas have developed library media program outcomes in alignment with *Information Power: Building Partnerships for Learning*, the National Goals 2000 effort and the Kansas Quality Performance Accreditation system. These newly drafted library media program outcomes support the concept of integrated instruction as proposed in the subject area curricular standards.

Recognizing the state's objectives as well as the national trend for LMSs to integrate information literacy outcomes into subject areas at all grade levels, the Kansas Association of School Librarians (KASL) Research Committee, in collaboration with the Kansas State Department of Education, embarked on a project to develop a model for assessing learning across the curriculum. From the earliest stages, plans called for the model to assess students' attainment of information skills as well as their curricular achievement. From 1994 to 1995, the KASL Research Committee conducted a literature review and developed the Preliminary 5-Step Model of the Handy 5 to facilitate such assessment, as shown in figure 8-1.

Figure 8-1 The Preliminary 5-Step Model of the Handy 5

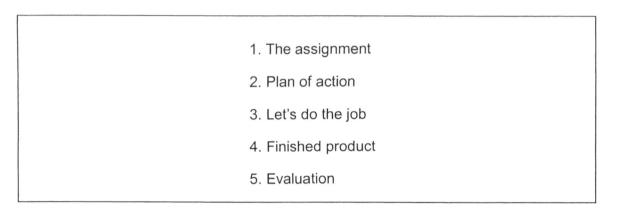

1. The assignment

2. Plan of action

3. Let's do the job

4. Finished product

5. Evaluation

During the summer of 1995, the committee organized a two-day summer institute to refine the model and to develop rubrics for assessing learning across the curriculum. Participating in development of the model were teachers, administrators, and Kansas State Department of Education curriculum specialists. In the fall of 1995, the Research Committee met to review and refine the model, including the rubrics for assessment. After revising the model, the committee members presented the model for reactions at six regional workshops sponsored by KASL. Feedback from these presentations was favorable and suggestions were incorporated into a second revision of the model in January 1996.

Two general research questions guided the project:

1. How does the model's usage facilitate student learning in selected grade levels and subject areas?

2. How does use of the model influence collaborative planning and integrated instruction?

The design of the study as well as the development of an integrated assessment model required (1) the establishment of a common language for LMSs to work with teachers in various curriculum areas, (2) a comparison of current state standards for subject areas, and (3) the creation of rubrics for each stage of the model. Each of these steps will be discussed in turn.

OVERVIEW OF THE STUDY

The KASL Research Committee identified Research Advisory Committee members from among the Kansas State Department of Education staff, school LMSs at various levels, subject area teachers, university faculty members, and school administrators. The Research Advisory Committee met twice in August 1996 to recommend research strategies and schools that might participate in the study. The Advisory Committee monitored the project through reports sent by the project chair to members.

To assist in the planning and implementation of the project, the Research Committee identified an independent research consultant, Dr. Delia Neuman, associate professor, College of Library and Information Services, University of Maryland. Dr. Neuman offered advice about the design of the study, the selection of research methods, and the selection of schools by participating by telephone in meetings of the Research Advisory Committee. She also participated by telephone in meetings of the researchers to address the researchers' questions regarding data collection techniques and the analysis of results.

SELECTING SCHOOLS

Schools were selected to assure diversity on each of the following criteria: (1) level (elementary, middle school, and high school); (2) size of school; (3) setting (rural, suburban, and urban); and (4) school climate (amount of integration of the teaching of information skills prior to the study). Participating LMSs agreed to be involved in the study both fall and spring semesters during the 1996 to 1997 school year and attend workshops at which the model was described and used.

Due to time constraints (all the researchers are employed in professional positions limiting their availability for travel and data collection), two categories of participating schools were established: self-reporting schools and case study schools. These two categories are discussed below.

Two of the researchers, a middle school LMS and an elementary school LMS, volunteered to participate as subjects of the study. These two researchers had been members of the committee that developed and revised the model and they were participants in the analysis of data obtained during the study. The middle school was designated a case study school, and the elementary school served as a self-reporting school. Selected for the study were ten schools, all representing the selection criteria: five elementary, one middle school, three high schools, and one K-12 school.

In consultation with the project consultant, the researchers agreed to concentrate efforts on three case study schools—one elementary, one middle, and one high school. One researcher was assigned to work with each case study school on a regular basis to visit, conduct interviews, and observe use of the model. During the fall semester the researchers observed lesson presentations and interviewed participating teachers and LMSs. The researchers also regularly contacted the LMSs by telephone. LMSs at seven self-reporting schools completed a School Information Form. Additionally, a "research partner" for each school (i.e., a member of the Research Committee) discussed the project with the LMS approximately every two weeks, using an interview guide. No school visits were made, but continuous monitoring of the model's use was accomplished through telephone contact. At the end of the fall semester, the researchers met to discuss the project; because the LMS at one of the sites had fallen ill, two of the seven original "self reporting" schools were designated "case study" schools for the spring semester. Additional observations and interviews were conducted for all schools during the spring semester.

RESEARCH METHODS

The Research Advisory Committee and the research consultant recommended research methods. Phone conferences with the research consultant were augmented by electronic mail communication and by faxed copies of instruments developed by the researchers. These refined instruments were created to gather data through interviews, classroom and library media center observations, lesson plans created at the sites, and school walkarounds.

Precise data-gathering instruments were required to ensure standardization of data collection by the team of researchers, who included one half-time elementary school LMS, two full-time elementary school LMSs, two high school LMSs, one graduate student, one state department consultant, and one library and information science school faculty member. One researcher was assigned to each of the ten participating schools. Researchers working with case study schools had that school as their only assignment, while researchers working with self-reporting schools had one or two schools assigned. Two of the participating LMSs (one elementary and one middle school) were members of the research committee but did not participate in the data collection; the elementary school was a self-reporting school, while the middle school was a case study. Data were gathered during the planning, implementation, and summative evaluation stages of units.

ANALYSIS OF DATA

Data were analyzed in three stages:

- an assessment midway through the study to review the data collection process;

- a preliminary analysis of results; and

- a thorough analysis by school.

During the first stage, the research team met at the conclusion of the fall semester of 1996 to review the data collection process and to analyze data collected to that point. The purpose of the analysis was to determine if the data collection techniques were adequate and to refine the data collection methods as necessary. Although the research team conferred by telephone on a monthly basis, synthesizing and analyzing the data provided an opportunity for all the researchers to see the study emerge as a whole. The interview and observation results, as well as lesson plans, were assembled by level of school and reviewed by teams of two or three researchers. Each team recorded the trends they saw emerging from their data. Collectively the researchers compared their findings and evaluated the data collection techniques. It was determined that the data collection methods were fulfilling the goals of the project, and no changes were made in the data collection process. However, an elementary and high school was changed from self-reporting to case study status in order to collect additional data.

During the second stage of analysis where the preliminary results were examined, the research team met at the conclusion of the spring semester of 1997 to analyze the data holistically. All the data were coded; the team divided into smaller groups to review the aggregated data, and the results were compiled into two categories corresponding to the two research questions:

1. How does the model's usage facilitate student learning in selected grade levels and subject areas?

2. How does use of the model influence collaborative planning and integrated instruction?

Based on a synthesis of the groups' analysis, the research team developed a list of preliminary findings. The researchers noted that data from the self-reporting schools were similar to that from the case study schools. Among the findings of this preliminary analysis was the need to clarify stages 4 (finished product) and 5 (evaluation) of the Handy 5. Another critical need that emerged was adaptation of the model for use with younger children.

The third stage of analysis began during the summer when two researchers (a senior university professor and a state department of education consultant) met over a period of several months to conduct a thorough analysis of the data by school. Quantitative data, including descriptive data collected routinely by the state department of education, and school profiles provided by the LMSs were combined with the qualitative interviews, observations, and lesson plans collected by researchers. The researchers compiled all the data by school and summarized the data for each. Then the researchers synthesized the summary findings, coding by school and topic.

OVERVIEW OF FINDINGS

The analysis of data from all of the participating schools yielded findings that fell into three categories:

- use of the model

- learning

- collaboration

These categories will be used as a framework for discussing findings from the research. Below is a summary of major findings, followed by a section that discusses the interpretation and evidence supporting each of them.

Use of the Handy 5

Research indicated that the model effectively provides a step-by-step framework for planning, building, and delivering a unit that integrates information skills and curricular content. Because this process is complex, LMSs can more effectively use the model with practice.

Learning

Following are additional findings regarding use of the model and its impact on student learning:

1. Use of the model had an impact on low-achieving students.

2. According to librarians and teachers, using the model helped students learn higher order thinking skills—i.e., analysis, synthesis, and evaluation.

3. Use of the model provided a framework for LMSs and teachers to assess student work in progress.

4. In classes that used the model, students found their work enjoyable.

5. In classes that used the model, students learned to approach the learning task systematically.

6. The model can be adapted for use with primary grade children.

Collaboration

The findings below indicate that the model is an effective tool in fostering collaboration among LMSs and teachers:

1. Use of the model can facilitate a transformation of the LMS's role to that of collaborating teacher of information skills.

2. Use of the model helps structure planning with teachers.

3. Use of the model is an efficient use of time.

4. Use of the model improves communication by establishing a common language.

5. Optimal use of the model requires a multi-faceted and ongoing continuing education program.

6. Optimal use of the model requires a school culture that supports collaboration.

Detailed Analysis: Use of the Handy 5

During the analysis of data, findings emerged in relation to each step of the model:

1. Assignment

2. Plan of action

3. Doing the job

4. Product evaluation

5. Process evaluation

The findings from the study support the integral nature of the model's five steps, emphasizing the systematic process required for successful teaching. Each step of the model feeds forward into the next steps, and all are linked. However, the process is not linear; for example, the assignment does not lead immediately to the plan of action. Instead, the teacher(s) may jump from a preliminary discussion of the assignment to exploration of the finished product; then return to the plan of action or to the assignment for further clarification.

Accompanying the findings below are statements providing evidence to support these results.

STEP 1: ASSIGNMENT

Finding: *Use of the model helps students to understand the assignment by helping them focus on project requirements.*

Evidence

At the beginning of a high school English unit, students were asked to write a paragraph stating their understanding of the assignment. Using the model rubric, the teacher scored the assignment step and noted that one student had written that she "didn't have a clue." The teacher then counseled the student individually, and the student went on to complete the assignment successfully.

An elementary LMS said: "Emphasis on the assignment being aligned with the finished product and evaluation really focuses the student learning."

Discussion

LMSs and teachers are sometimes prone to overestimate students' ability to comprehend an assignment. That is, educators tend to give credit for students' understanding of an assignment even when students do not in fact understand the intent of the assignment and the expectations of the teachers for it. Typically, teachers and LMSs do not probe for students' understanding of the assignment.

STEP 2: PLAN OF ACTION

Finding: *The "plan of action" is the critical link between the assignment and the successful finished product.*

Evidence

A high school LMS explained that, without instruction, many students go directly to terminals and start searching the Internet. They don't consider which is the best source to try; they tend to use the same search techniques regardless of their needs, believing that the Internet will have what they need. The LMS added that the students, having completed the unit using the model, wasted less time; they planned strategically for finding information.

A fourth-grade teacher also said that the plan of action was the most useful part of the model: "Especially working with little kids—this step by step part is helpful."

Discussion

Without a carefully considered plan of action, students will often plunge into the search for information without using information skills.

STEP 3: DOING THE JOB

Finding: *"Doing the Job" is an integral stage in the learning process.*

Evidence

One of the researchers called a LMS to check on progress of fourth graders on a science unit. When the researcher suggested a date to visit, the LMS said, "You're welcome to come then, but the students are only working on their science projects."

Discussion

Educators often require students to complete an assignment outside class time, or they consider in-class time for doing the job unimportant, as indicated in the example above. In this example the LMS was saying that nothing important was happening; the assignment had been given, and information search strategies had been developed, but there was no product to evaluate. The students were "only" working on the projects to complete the assignment. This research shows that each step of the process is linked with each of the other steps; like a five-legged "footstool," if one leg is removed, the stool will be unsteady and may fall over. "Doing the job" must not be overlooked or given low priority by teachers and LMSs; it should be monitored and assessed like the other four steps of the Handy 5.

STEPS 4 AND 5: PRODUCT AND PROCESS EVALUATION

Finding: *As LMSs began to use the model, they had difficulty discerning the difference between evaluating the finished product and evaluating the learning process.*

Evidence

Of the nine schools that implemented the model, five reported difficulty in general in the evaluation. All five are elementary schools. The four schools that reported no difficulty in the evaluation phase or in using the rubrics had extensive exposure to the model. Two of these schools were staffed by LMSs who were members of the Research Committee, and the other two schools were staffed by LMSs who had attended workshops at which the model was taught.

An elementary school LMS told the researcher that she struggled with the evaluation step of the model. She defined evaluation as the "product evaluation" stage and had omitted the "process evaluation" stage.

Evaluation worked better with the second attempt (second unit). The LMS thought this could be due to the more collaborative relationship between the teacher and LMS and to development of rubrics by students.

Discussion

Teachers generally consider the finished product the culminating activity for a unit (e.g., paper, project, oral report, etc.). They provide for an evaluation of this product, usually in the form of a numerical or letter grade, but neither they nor their students always evaluate the process of building the product. This situation is analogous to completing a trip and assessing the destination without evaluating the travel as part of the trip experience.

Evaluation is a complex process, and continuing education is needed for teachers and LMSs to implement effective assessment of student learning. The difficulty of assessment is illustrated by incidents from the study.

GENERAL STATEMENTS ABOUT THE HANDY 5

Following are findings that related to the model as a whole, and not to any one or two particular steps of the model.

Finding: *The model provides a step-by-step framework for planning, building, and delivering a unit.*

Evidence

An elementary school LMS said, "Checking along the way we're not good at yet because that's not traditional. We assess at the end traditionally. Having the steps for assessment makes us aware of teaching a total understanding before we go on. Before, we rammed them through and tested at the end."

An elementary LMS noted that she now has "a plan of attack"—the model provides a framework for planning a unit.

Discussion

The Handy 5 was developed as a tool to help LMSs and teachers assess both information literacy and learning in various subject areas and at all grade levels. An expected finding of the study was the importance of the model as a tool for developing and implementing a unit of instruction.

Finding: *The unit-building process is complex, and LMSs can use the model more effectively with practice.*

Evidence

After using the model twice, the LMS said she felt better prepared to present the model to students.

An elementary LMS discussed the model: "The more I use it, the more sense it makes. It makes me feel that we're covering a concept more thoughtfully and more carefully trying to teach all parts before going on . . . . It takes time and planning. We have to rethink how we do things . . . . Now I'm willing to be venturesome and try it again with other teachers."

Discussion

LMSs cannot effectively use the model after reading about it or hearing only a single presentation about it. Needed is practice using the model, based on careful reading of this book. It is helpful for LMSs to discuss with other colleagues the teaching process and use of the model in order to plan, teach, and evaluate units effectively. There is no magic bullet for gaining expertise; it must be developed through extensive practice over time.

Detailed Analysis: Learning

Finding: *Use of the model had an impact on low-achieving students.*

Evidence

One elementary teacher who had provided the students with the opportunity to develop rubrics for the model reported that students had a complete understanding of the assignment, were 100% of the time on task, and created a high quality finished product as a result of rubric development and use. These were "low-achieving" students, described by the teacher as "difficult students."

Discussion

The research demonstrated that the model was workable with students at all grades and levels of ability.

Finding: *According to librarians and teachers, using the model helped students to learn higher order thinking skills—i.e., analysis, synthesis, and evaluation.*

Evidence

An elementary school LMS said:

> Using a rubric is more specific than using a letter grade or a percentage. Assessing the assignment, doing the job, or the integrated finished product allows the student to have feedback throughout the entire project. This process feedback helps focus teacher and student attention on the desired outcomes. In the student and teacher evaluations, the finished products were more complete. The rubric helps the students understand their own strengths for the next project, and what areas they are weak in, so that they can improve. Feedback and assessment throughout the project helps student organization also. The emphasis on aligning the assignments with the assessment from planning through evaluation made for a more cohesive learning experience. We have also seen improvement in students using these assessed skills when required to complete assignments in other learning situations.

Middle school students were not accustomed to self-evaluation and looking at their end products for areas in which they could improve the end result. Most were accustomed to a process of "just finish it, hand it in and be done with it."

In an elementary school classroom observation, a researcher determined that student involvement in rubric design had a positive impact on successful project completion. After the students completed the self-check, it was reviewed by the LMS and teacher, who agreed that the students accurately self-reported their evaluations.

The researcher observed during classroom observations that several second-grade students reported on the same planets. Sometimes the number of moons for a planet varied among the reports. Students never challenged each other; instead they challenged the information source, which indicates that they were learning evaluation or analytical skills.

Discussion

One of the important trends in education is to teach through simple recognition and recall, more than the basic skills of reading, writing, and arithmetic. In today's fast-changing society, students must learn to think critically and to apply knowledge from the disciplines to unforeseen real-world problems. The research indicated that use of the model facilitated the teaching and learning of analysis, synthesis, and evaluation skills.

Finding: *The model helped LMSs and teachers to assess student work in progress.*

Evidence

An elementary LMS said, "For evaluation, we each set up rubrics from the model. We felt that these rubrics helped students understand what areas they were weak or strong in so that they could use that information towards successful projects in the future. We found that when students look at a rubric their assessment is much easier for them to understand and use than just a letter or percentage grade."

During the end-of-year interview, an elementary school LMS said that before using the model she couldn't assess how well students use information; now she can do that.

Discussion

Traditionally, LMSs are not engaged in the assessment of student learning. Use of the Handy 5 not only engaged the LMS in assessment, it enabled the assessment of the entire learning process; the assessment was formative as well as summative.

Finding: *Students found their work enjoyable.*

Evidence

One elementary LMS found it rewarding to have the students "dig in" and never indicate frustration with the process—no whining occurred; instead, students asked questions out of genuine curiosity and were willing to make corrections and check the accuracy of information. The LMS believed the students had fun with this project.

High school students were involved, took notes, and asked questions. They appeared to have a good time doing the chemistry project.

The fourth-grade teacher told the LMS: "What would have been a drudgery project was exciting and very successful." The students were enthusiastic, involved, and proud of their work.

The model made a difference in that it relieved high school students' anxiety and frustration; they had a clearer understanding of how to proceed.

Discussion

Learning need not be arduous or puzzling. Indeed, learning can be a joy. Educators must provide a framework and an inviting environment that encourage enjoyment. The Handy 5 helps provide such a framework and environment.

Finding: *Students learned to approach the learning task systematically.*

Evidence

A middle school LMS said, "This seemed to be the first time that this type of information process had been taught and used by this group of students. They appeared to see some importance in following this system of information seeking while at the same time questioning why they had to spend time planning their search. They seemed accustomed to just jumping into a project without preplanning and often not even knowing where they wanted to go or what the finished product would be."

The sixth-grade teacher said students were able to focus on their expectations. She did not solve problems for the students; she reminded them of the timeline—then walked away. In the past, the assignments came from the textbook, and students did not have "personal ownership." This time, they did have ownership, which was verified by comments they made during the evaluation of the unit.

An elementary school LMS said: "Emphasis on the assignment being aligned with the finished product and evaluation really focuses the student learning."

A sixth-grade social studies student teacher observed that the model helped students think of each step of the process instead of thinking only of the finished product.

A high school teacher and LMS shared with the researcher that the model was the "backbone" of a high school chemistry unit. Some of the better students said in the evaluations that they felt slowed down because they had already internalized this process of learning. However, the model worked with most of the students, enabling them to understand the learning process better.

Discussion

Learning is a process that must be practiced, yet many students are unaware of this process. The Handy 5 identifies a five-step process for teaching and learning that can be directly taught to students.

Finding: *The model can be adapted for use with primary grade children.*

Evidence

An elementary school LMS recommended that the model be taught in small chunks. Teaching it as a whole process does not work well below fourth grade. She used all steps of the model and in step 5 used a simplified language, developed in collaboration with the teacher.

Discussion

The Handy 5 represents a learning process that can work for students of all ages; however, some of the terms adopted for the model are not readily recognizable by younger students. Research shows that the model can work for all ages but should be adapted for use with primary grade children.

Detailed Analysis: Collaboration

Finding: *Use of the model facilitates a transformation of the LMS's role to that of collaborating teacher of information skills.*

Evidence

An elementary LMS said, "We assessed each [third grade] child separately, then compared our assessments. When comparing the rubric results and comments, we found we had a very complete picture of each child's ability to read and use information! The results will be beneficial in other research projects and were shared with the reading specialist for students we felt needed extra help. We will also use this information to design learning activities to increase the skill levels for use of information and expository reading comprehension."

Using the model made it easier to plan, teach, and evaluate student work in a high school. The teacher and LMS equally shared teaching for both units. They shared teaching to the extent that each felt comfortable contributing to the discussion the other person was leading.

When planning with the LMS, one elementary school teacher said she "came up with even better ideas . . . I enjoy working with other staff members as a team."

Discussion

The national standards and professional literature for LMSs promote the role of the LMS as a collaborator with teachers in the teaching of information skills; however, experience of the researchers suggests that most LMSs assist teachers as unequal partners. Instead of being co-designers of instruction, many LMSs are supplemental to instruction. Seldom are LMSs involved in either the planning or the assessment of instruction. Often the role of the LMS focuses on the acquisition, organization, retrieval, and circulation of resources, with little integrated, cross-disciplinary teaching of information skills.

Finding: *Use of the model helps structure planning with teachers.*

Evidence

One elementary LMS had a limited amount of experience collaborating, and the model provided her with helpful guidelines.

A middle school LMS commented that the model was "a guideline for helping decide what to do and for scheduling." When she taught from the model, it simplified the teaching by keeping her focused.

A high school teacher noted that a strength of the model is that it facilitates working with other teachers so that everyone knows where to begin planning. It gives the teachers a "safety net," like a textbook, to follow.

Discussion

While the model provides a structure for learning, as noted above, it also provides a framework for planning with teachers. The research indicates that the model was a valuable tool to assist LMSs and teachers in the planning of integrated information skills instruction.

Finding: *Use of the model is an efficient use of time.*

Evidence

An elementary school LMS said, "The more I use [the model] the more convinced I am it's effective and time saving."

A high school LMS said that using the model is a good use of time, which is a factor for teachers. Teachers are reluctant to give their time for collaborative planning, but once they do, they see the value.

Discussion

Teachers and LMSs are very busy people, and time is a precious commodity. There is never enough time to accomplish all of the tasks that need to be done; yet the school schedule usually does not provide adequate time for planning. Teachers are reluctant to engage in any new activity that requires an investment of additional time; however, the Handy 5 appears to be a productive use of time.

Finding: *Use of the model improves communication by establishing a common language.*

Evidence

An elementary LMS said, "We found that our plan time with all teaching professionals was more effective due to the common language of the model. It facilitated combining objectives very well. Integrated planning allowed us to add research and information skills, quality literature, artistic design, writing skills, speech, and storytelling skills to the social studies objectives."

   A researcher observed that the high school LMS had a large pool of volunteers to choose from, but she selected for the research project teachers with whom she knew she could work effectively. She worked with English and chemistry teachers, recognizing they represented disparate subject areas, and she perceived that one of the strengths of the model might be its ease in facilitating work with very different subject areas.

Discussion

In order for LMSs to work with teachers across subject areas, the LMS must be able to use teachers' language to communicate. The Handy 5 provides the language of several disciplines for this integrated planning.

Finding: *Use of the model requires a multi-faceted and ongoing continuing education program.*

Evidence

A middle school LMS said, "We feel that this process will improve with continued use and that the process would be best if started in early elementary and built on at each grade level. Only with repetition and by using this process in early research will this be as effective a process as possible. It would be best if taught to all teachers and used as a school district process. It also needs times for planning, teaching and reteaching, and teachers who are receptive to its use and willing to take the time to use it."

Discussion

Successful implementation of the model requires LMSs to implement a long-range plan for continuing education of their teachers. The model takes time to learn, and a part of the learning is practice of its use. Another component is reflection on successes and failures during implementation. Implementation of interdisciplinary, integrated information skills instruction is an ongoing process requiring workshops or other continuing education activities to impart new teaching and assessment techniques.

Finding: *Implementation of the model is easier in a school culture that supports collaboration.*

Evidence

A researcher reported the following:
    The model was not implemented in one of the self-reporting schools. In this instance, the LMS was in her first year as a high school librarian in a new school, following several years as an elementary school LMS.
    The biggest problem the LMS discovered was building a teaching relationship with the teachers in the high school. The school climates in an elementary, middle school, junior high, and high school are different in their relationships among teachers, students, and the content learned. The LMS summed up the difference between elementary and high schools as follows: "Elementary teachers own the kids; high school teachers own the curriculum." The LMS felt that sharing the role of teacher does not come easily for high school teachers. The high school teachers seemed not to see the need for sharing the teacher role, and the LMS felt that the library was not seen as an integral part of the teaching process of the building. The LMS felt that she was not involved in the curriculum planning and was therefore at a disadvantage. The LMS believed that, if she had been able to interject bits and pieces into ongoing projects of the classroom teachers, she might have been able to do something with the model.

Discussion

This finding supports the research of Grover (1996), who wrote: "School culture must support collaboration" (p. 3). Sites were selected for the study based in part on LMS participation and school support. In one case, the LMS changed schools before the research project was initiated, and the environment was not conducive to collaboration or to implementing the Handy 5.

IMPLICATIONS FOR PRACTICE

The role of the LMS goes beyond building collections, providing Internet access, and scheduling programs; the new role is that of emphasizing instructional partnering, teaching, and assessing learning. The LMS should be engaged as a collaborative partner in the teaching process as part of the attempt to structure a learner-centered school.
    A key element of a learner-centered school is continuous assessment of student performance, and integrated assessments require collaboration among all educators—administrators, teachers, LMSs, and staff. More than a cosmetic change, a collaborative school culture to support integrated assessment requires a substantive change in school culture and the way that schools "do business." Our research shows that the Handy 5 provides an effective tool for LMSs and teachers to use to collaborate and to implement change.
    One of the problems that LMSs have had in shifting from a traditional supportive role to one of collaboration was the lack of a framework for collaboration—missing were the tools that could assist the LMS in this teaching role with subject area specialists. Although models for collaboration have been developed by Turner (1993) and by Cleaver and Taylor (1989), these models did not have steps of the teaching process, and they did not provide rubrics for assessment. In the past, LMS's did not have the specialized subject area knowledge, the vocabulary, or the assessment skills to plan, build, and evaluate instructional units. The KASL Research Committee, with assistance from teachers, administrators, LMSs, university faculty, and state-level consultants, developed the Handy 5 to address the need for tools to help LMSs and teachers work together effectively as teaching teams. Feedback from the professional community and results of the committee's research indicate that the Handy 5 is effective as a planning guide, as an assessment tool, and as a learning aid for students.

STRENGTHS OF THE MODEL

This suggests that the model can have a positive impact on student learning and that it can be used with all grade levels and all abilities. The framework provided by the model helped students to learn higher order thinking skills—i.e., analysis, synthesis, and evaluation. The model provided support and structure for LMSs and teachers to assess student work in progress, thereby encouraging students to approach the learning task systematically. Our research also showed that using the model resulted in students' finding their work enjoyable.

The research findings indicate that the model is an effective tool in fostering collaboration among LMSs and teachers. The model facilitates a transformation of the LMS's role to that of collaborating teacher of information skills. Use of the model is an efficient use of time because it structures planning with teachers and improves communication by using a common language.

NEEDS ASSOCIATED WITH USE OF THE MODEL

Implementation of the model requires a school culture that supports collaboration, otherwise teachers will reject the concept of integrating information skills instruction across the curriculum. Furthermore, implementation of the model requires multifaceted and ongoing preservice and continuing education programs because of the complexity of the teaching and assessing process. To be used effectively with primary grade children, the Handy 5 must be adapted so that the language is suitable for younger children.

SUMMARY

This chapter summarized the research results conducted by school LMSs and by state department and university personnel. The research is qualitative in nature and demonstrated that the Handy 5 is a useful tool for planning and assessing learning.

The Handy 5 research is still relevant and applicable to the work of the LMS. Donald Adcock and Patricia Montiel-Overall, co-editors of the *Best of Knowledge Quest*, the first in a new series published by the American Association of School Librarians, note:

> The purpose of the series is to combine into a single publication a select number of outstanding articles on a topic of current interest to the profession that has appeared in *Knowledge Quest* during the past several years. The topic of the first publication is the series on collaboration. The article "Planning and Assessing Learning Across the Curriculum," by the Kansas Association of School Librarians Research Committee was selected to be included in the publication. The articles included in this publication address three areas of interest: research, best practice and articles that present an overview of the topic. (Adcock, 2006)

The authors of *The Handy 5* are pleased that their research is withstanding the test of time. Also, they are impressed with the application of the model for use with young children. The work of Jan Stover to adapt the five steps for use by the Pre-K is a major achievement.

REFERENCES

Adcock, Donald and Patricia Montiel-Overall. E-mail mesaage to Dr. Bob Grover, July 2006.

American Association of School Librarians and Association for Educational Communications and Technology. *Information Power: Building Partnerships for Learning.* Chicago: American Library Association, 1998.

Cleaver, Betty P. and William D. Taylor. *The Instructional Consultant Role of the School Library Media Specialist.* Chicago and London: American Library Association, 1989.

Grover, Robert. *Collaboration.* Chicago: American Association of School Librarians, 1996.

Turner, Phillip M. *Helping Teachers Teach: A School Library Media Specialist's Role.* Englewood, CA: Libraries Unlimited, 1993.

PART THREE

The Model in Action

9

Sample Lesson Plans

Elementary School Examples

Middle School Examples

High School Examples

During the design, field-testing, and implementation of the Handy 5, many library media specialists requested sample unit plans. Some examples were produced by workshop trainers and participants and some were the result of work at field-testing sites. Also, some members of the research team-taught library media courses for universities and their students completed assignments using the Handy 5. These groups and their students willingly provided model unit plans in a variety of subjects and grade levels for this book. University students were encouraged to make use of online teacher lesson sites as a beginning stage for their units. While they were instructed to give credit for their citations, the amount of adaptation makes it a fuzzy area as to whether the online plan is fully credited. The editor of this publication takes no responsibility for this matter. The KASLS research/writing teams hope these examples will assist the LMS in implementing this model at the local level. The examples in this chapter are presented in K–12 order. A blank form for unit planning is also included.

The first few unit examples follow The Primary 3 Model and are focused on literature and likely are not going to be collaborative units, but support for a reading program. There are also examples from primary grades that are collaborative units focused on classroom content and use all of the five steps.

The standard and benchmark numbers may not align with your particular curriculum objectives because the lesson plans have come from various sources—local, state, and national documents. For the purpose of these examples, the focused standards have been limited to a minimum of two. So don't limit using the plans at only the standards indicated.

Thanks go to the following people for their help:

Courtney Ast	Denise Irwin
Elsa Barrio	Lisa Johnson
Tammi Benham	Betsy Losey
Nancy Cudney	Ellie Seeman
Lisa Dewane	Melissa Sipe
Jill Dodge	J.K. Stover
Nina Flax	Beverly Troglia
Carol Fox	Nicole Unruh
Mandy Fritz	Shirley Vogts
Shirley Hargis	Karen Wilson
Karla Hawver	Stacy Youngberg

Collaborative Planning Outline

<table>
<tr><td>

Standards Accomplished Addressed
Where does this assignment fit? What curriculum objectives will it fulfill?

1. Library Media Standards:

2. Collaborative Content Standards:

</td></tr>
</table>

Level: **Teacher's Name:**
Title:
Time to Be Completed:

One-Sentence Summary of the Assignment: What is the student to do? (Step 1) What will he have to show for it? (Step 4)

Finished Product Evaluation: What are the criteria and method by which the student will be graded? (Step 4)

Plan of Action: What activities will be used to reach the assignment outcomes? What new information will need to be presented? (Step 2)

Library Media Specialist	**Classroom Teacher**
a.	a.
b.	b.
c.	c.

Notes about Doing the Job: How is the unit developing; is the plan working? (Step 3)

Process Evaluation: How well did it go, what should be done differently next time? Documentation for student achievement, i.e., % of students reaching benchmark. (Step 5)

Student Assessment Measures: (Student product that assesses each step)
1. Assignment—
2. Plan of Action—
3. Doing the Job—
4. Product Evaluation—
5. Process Evaluation—

Materials/Resources: Include only special requirements.

Plan of Action: Individual Lesson

Objective: (For today's lesson. There can be as many or as few objectives as necessary to do a day's lesson)

Introduction: (Engaging students in the learning)

Activity 1: (Description of the way learning is to occur—may or may not be assessed at this time)

Activity 2: (Description of the way learning is to occur—may or may not be assessed at this time)

Assessment: (May be done at a later date)

Student Reflection: (How is this going to help me to do the assignment, what was new today, etc.)

Teacher Reflection: (How well did the lesson go?)

Collaborative Planning Outline   **Pre-K-Kindergarten—The Handy 3**

Standards Accomplished Addressed
Where does this assignment fit? What curriculum objectives will it fulfill?

1. **Library Media Standards:**
   Standard 1: The student who is information literate accesses information efficiently and effectively.
   Benchmark 2: The student recognizes that accurate and comprehensive information is the basis for intelligent decision making.

2. **Collaborative Content Standards:**
   Reading:
   Standard 1: The student reads and comprehends text across the curriculum.
   Benchmark 1: The student uses skills in alphabetics to construct meaning from text.

Level: Pre-K & Kindergarten reading   **Teacher's Name:**
Title: "The Fishy Letter Game (Pre-Skill for Story Sequencing)"
Time to Be Completed: One 20-minute session

One-Sentence Summary of the Assignment: What is the student to do? (Step 1) What will he have to show for it? (Step 4)

Students will identify names of both upper and lower case letters of the alphabet and place them in sequence.

Finished Product Evaluation: What are the criteria and method by which the student will be graded? (Step 4)

- Student uses the alphabet line on the wall and recite the letters in alpha order to play the game of sorting the letters on each fish-shaped game piece. May also sing the *Alphabet Song* before placing the card/alphabet fish in the correct bowl.
- Student checks each fish bowl for accuracy after the game cards are sorted.
- Student uses the terms of Beginning, Middle, and End to describe the three fish bowls (A-G, H-N, and O-Z). They are color-coded the same as the Handy 3.

Plan of Action: What activities will be used to reach the assignment outcomes? What new information will need to be presented? (Step 2)

Library Media Specialist	**Classroom Teacher**
a. Create the game pieces and set up and maintain the game area.	a. Maintain the game and assign the cards for each student.
b. Explain rules and order of play.	b. Keep the game pace fast by having cards ready for the next player.
c. Review the skills at end of game and compare the game organization to the Handy 3 Primary Model.	c. Return the game to the class area.

Notes about Doing the Job: How is the unit developing, is the plan working? (Step 3)

Cut lower fin off of the tag board fish game pieces in order to identify the top fin portion of the fish. It will help the students identify the correct position of the letter. Not every student will need to recite the *Alphabet Song* in order to match the letter to the corresponding bowl.

Process Evaluation: How well did it go; what should be done differently next time? Documentation for student achievement, i.e., % of students reaching benchmark. (Step 5)

Could do a sample exercise with fish bowls that have only 5 letters per bowl to sort (A-D, F-J, etc.). Place all the letters on the bowl (very small) on the back of the bowl for self-checking when it is used in the classroom.

Student Assessment Measures: (Student product that assesses each step)
1. Assignment—Sort alphabet cards into corresponding fish bowls.
2. Plan of Action—
3. Doing the Job—Students play the Fishy Letter Game.
4. Product Evaluation—
5. Process Evaluation—Check the alphabet fish cards in each bowl by matching them with the alphabet on display in the classroom.

Materials/Resources: Include only special requirements.

Adapted from the game "Dictionary Go Fish," page 47, *Stretch Library Lessons: Research Skills* by Pat Miller; small plastic fish bowls, alphabet letter strips on display, tag board letter fish with upper and lower case letters printed on the front of the cards

Plan of Action: Individual Lesson

Objective: (For today's lesson. There can be as many or as few objectives as necessary to do a day's lesson.)
Student will use printed alphabet cards with upper and lower case letters and sort the letter "fish" into the correct fish bowl.

Introduction: (Engaging students in the learning.)
Sing the *Alphabet Song* with the students. Read letters left to right from the alphabet letter chart. Cover up several letters and ask them if they know which letters are missing.

Activity 1: (Description of the way learning is to occur–may or may not be assessed at this time.)
Introduce the Fishy Letter Game to the students. Student will select a fish from the pond, tell the class what letter he selected, bring it up to the fish bowl, and place it in the matching bowl. Student will quietly "swim" back to his or her seat.

Activity 2: (Description of the way learning is to occur–may or may not be assessed at this time.)

Assessment: (May be done at a later date.)
Check the letter card order by placing them in alphabetical order up on the letter chart or by singing the *Alphabet Song.*

Student Reflection: (How is this going to help me to do the assignment, what was new today, etc.)
Students had fun singing, fishing, and learning with the alphabet. It was nice to take the game back to the classroom and play it again during center time.

Teacher Reflection: (How well did the lesson go?)
Might be fun to have students in two lines in front of fish bowls. They can go fishing when it is their turn to select a random card from the "pond" pile that is located in between the two lines.

Collaborative Planning Outline   **Kindergarten–1st Grade—The Handy 3**

Standards Accomplished Addressed
Where does this assignment fit? What curriculum objectives will it fulfill?

1. **Library Media Standards:**
   Standard 2: The student who is information literate evaluates information critically and competently.
   Standard 3: The student who is information literate uses information accurately and creatively.

2. **Collaborative Content Standards:**
   Reading:
   Standard 2: The student responds to a variety of text.
   Benchmark 1: The student uses literary concepts to interpret and respond to text.

Level: Kindergarten–1st grade reading   **Teacher's Name:**
Title: "What Is Olivia Working on Now?"
Time to Be Completed: One 30-minute session

One-Sentence Summary of the Assignment: What is the student to do? (Step 1) What will he have to show for it? (Step 4)

Students will use visual, auditory, and spatial cues to problem-solve with the main character to help create and complete a Handy 3 graphic organizer, using it as they re-tell the story.

Finished Product Evaluation: What are the criteria and method by which the student will be graded? (Step 4)

- Student identifies the problem in the story.
- Student composes sentences and put story picture cards in sequential order, using the color-coded train cars.
- Student uses the picture cards in order to retell the story using graphic organizer.

Plan of Action: What activities will be used to reach the assignment outcomes? What new information will need to be presented? (Step 2)

Library Media Specialist	**Classroom Teacher**
a. Review the story map chart and introduce the color-coded Handy 3 boxcar.	a. Present and reinforce sequencing skills.
b. Read the story aloud and use the picture cards to help organize and re-tell the action of the main character in the story.	b. Introduce story sequence chart, story mapping, and problem-solving chart.

Notes about Doing the Job: How is the unit developing; is the plan working? (Step 3)

Picture cards are displayed on the storyboard in random order. It helps to have a flannel board and use hook and loop fasteners to allow students to arrange the pictures in order on the board. Some students prefer to pick up the picture cards from the floor and place them in the boxcar baskets that form the train. Allow students to choose the method of arranging the picture cards.

Process Evaluation: How well did it go, what should be done differently next time? Documentation for student achievement, i.e., % of students reaching benchmark. (Step 5)

Students can review parts of a story by using the graphic organizer used in the classroom. This organizer allows students to see the actions of the main character in the story flow from the beginning where the problem is stated, to the middle where steps are taken to solve the problem and finally to the end where the solution is formed.

Student Assessment Measures: (Student product that assesses each step)
1. Assignment—Identify which picture card depicts the problem that the main character needs to solve.
2. Plan of Action—Students place the picture cards in order as they happen in the story.
3. Doing the Job—Students place the cards in the color-coded boxcar that follows the Handy 3 steps.
4. Product Evaluation—Have students determine that the order of the story cards is in the right sequence by reviewing the pictures in the book.
5. Process Evaluation—Students show approval or disapproval with thumbs up or thumbs down to vote on how the main character solved the problem. A level thumb or no vote may mean that the student has a suggestion about how the problem could have been solved differently.

Materials/Resources: Include only special requirements.

Create story sequence cards by using actual photos from the book. Glue the copy on construction paper and laminate. Use the book *Olivia and the Missing Toy*, by Ian Falconer for the story sequence lesson. Other titles that could be used to introduce the main character are *Olivia, Olivia Saves the Circus, Olivia Forms a Band*, also by Falconer.

Plan of Action: Individual Lesson

Objective: (For today's lesson. There can be as many or as few objectives as necessary to do a day's lesson.)
Students will use a story map, sequence chart, problem solution chart, or the Handy 3 organizer to reinforce the story elements of sequencing, story order, and main character.

Introduction: (Engaging students in the learning.)
Introduce the main character in the series of stories. Read a few of the stories before introducing this lesson in order to assist students in understanding the concept of a main character. Olivia is an exciting little pig that has painted a masterpiece, saved a circus, and is now working on her latest problem in *Olivia and the Missing Toy*.

Activity 1: (Description of the way learning is to occur–may or may not be assessed at this time.)
When reading the story to the group, point out details in the illustrations as you read. Make sure that the selected picture cards are up so everyone in the group can see them. Use of the color-coded sticky notes or markers while reading will help set up the organization of the story map and the connection to the Handy 3 process of problem-solving.

Activity 2: (Description of the way learning is to occur–may or may not be assessed at this time.)
Pre-readers will use picture cards to help retell the story after it is read aloud. Selected pictures chosen from the story should help divide the story using the story map graphic organizer and the train organizer. There may be more than one picture in each section of the story. The book will be used to check the story card order. Students will use oral skills to choose pictures for the boxcars or story map, instead of pointing to the picture without verbalization.

Student Reflection: (How is this going to help me to do the assignment, what was new today, etc.)
Students seemed to enjoy noticing the details of the story and successfully placed the picture cards as they appeared in the book.

Teacher Reflection: (How well did the lesson go?)
Many pre-readers have difficulty expressing their thoughts. However, they need to be encouraged to use their words instead of simply pointing to the picture cards. Use of the train baskets on the floor is helpful to keep younger students moving and actively participating in the retelling of the story.

Collaborative Planning Outline   **Kindergarten–2nd Grade—The Handy 3**

Standards Accomplished Addressed
Where does this assignment fit? What curriculum objectives will it fulfill?

1. **Library Media Standards:**
   Standard 5: The student who is an independent learner is information literate and appreciates literature and other creative expressions of information.

2. **Collaborative Content Standards:**
   Literature:
   Standard 2: The student responds to a variety of text.
   Benchmark 1:The student uses literary concepts to interpret and respond to text.

Level: Kindergarten–2nd grade literature   **Teacher's Name:**
Title: "Arthur's Nose"
Time to Be Completed: Four 30-minute sessions

One-Sentence Summary of the Assignment: What is the student to do? (Step 1) What will he have to show for it? (Step 4)

After using the website for author/illustrator Marc Brown, and other print resources, students will make a poster of Arthur showing his ever-changing nose; they will make their own new nose to use for a photo collage of all their classmates' new noses.

Finished Product Evaluation: What are the criteria and method by which the student will be graded? (Step 4)

- Student demonstrates accuracy of information presented in the posters.
- Student demonstrates recognition of how the main character is illustrated in a variety of print resources and attention to detail by research of the provided resources.
- Student demonstrates an expression of the artistic changes in the photographs and drawings created by the students to show how the illustrator made changes to the main character through the years.

Plan of Action: What activities will be used to reach the assignment outcomes? What new information will need to be presented? (Step 2)

Library Media Specialist

a. Introduce Marc Brown.
b. Teach lesson on elements of design and detail.
c. Read several stories to show changes in character's appearance.
d. Prepare materials for the student activities.

Classroom Teacher

a. Assist in the collection of books that show changes in character's appearance.
b. Take digital photos of students with their new noses.
c. Assist students with class photo collage poster.

Notes about Doing the Job: How is the unit developing; is the plan working? (Step 3)

The posters can take longer than expected to complete. However, it is important to encourage students to finish their artwork according to the directions given by the teacher so that the pictures will appear colorful and bold in the photos placed on the collage.

Process Evaluation: How well did it go, what should be done differently next time? Documentation for student achievement, i.e., % of students reaching benchmark. (Step 5)

This lesson would be most effective if the teacher or library media specialist would define and introduce the job of an illustrator and an author before this lesson is presented.

Student Assessment Measures: (Student product that assesses each step)
1. Assignment—Students will make drawings of Arthur's nose and a photo collage of their own noses.
2. Plan of Action—Variety of books, pictures, and resources are reviewed and made available for students' use.
3. Doing the Job—Creating the drawings and photo collage.
4. Product Evaluation—Drawings created by students reflect the guidelines of the assignment and photo collage.
5. Process Evaluation—Class discussion about the creating and presentation of the drawings and collage.

Materials/Resources: Include only special requirements.

Cut white construction paper for the sketches at 4" x 11". Teacher will need a digital camera, and a media presentation cart with web access. Web access may be substituted with materials and information found in the 25th Anniversary Edition of Marc Brown's book: *Arthur's Nose*. This book has resources that can be used to present the information found on the website. Overhead masters or enlargements of the pictures, letters and fun facts presented in the book will make an interesting bulletin board presentation for the students. Other books to use to introduce the illustrations and author Marc Brown's character Arthur the aardvark: *Arthur's Nose, Arthur's Valentine, Arthur's April Fool, Arthur's Teacher Trouble, Arthur Babysits,* and *Arthur's Computer Disaster.*

Plan of Action: Individual Lesson

Objective: (For today's lesson. There can be as many or as few objectives as necessary to do a day's lesson.)
Introduce the concept of the job of an illustrator and author. Present a variety of materials to the students that show the elements of detail and design while informing them about the life and work of Marc Brown and his famous character Arthur the aardvark.

Introduction: (Engaging students in the learning.)
Read several books by Marc Brown that feature Arthur. Present information from the video and print resources to the students. Visit the Marc Brown website and see pictures of the author, read letters and frequently asked questions, and play a few games. While the LMS introduces the author, the teacher can add information to the bulletin board display.

Activity 1: (Description of the way learning is to occur–may or may not be assessed at this time.)
After students have been introduced to a variety of print, video, and web resources, they may begin to sketch out their ideas for a new nose after listening to the story *Arthur's Nose* by Marc Brown.

Activity 2: (Description of the way learning is to occur–may or may not be assessed at this time.)
Students will check in with the teacher and make refinements to the sketches. When the drawing is complete they will have their picture taken with their new nose creation. The photographs will be added to the poster collage and placed on a wall display or on a bulletin board.

Assessment: (May be done at a later date.)
Students are tested statewide on skills in alphabetics, understanding of concepts of print, determining meaning of unknown words or phrases using picture cues and context clues. Review of these skills is very helpful to a successful reading program.

Student Reflection: (How is this going to help me to do the assignment, what was new today, etc.)
Provides a visual marker for students to see how the information is being used to answer content questions about the story.

Teacher Reflection: (How well did the lesson go?)
I might expand the drawing activity and bind all of the pictures of the many noses in a flipbook and place a cover on each of them. Give a copy of the book to each teacher to use in a reading center in the classroom.

Collaborative Planning Outline   **Grades One–Three—The Handy 3**

Standards Accomplished Addressed
Where does this assignment fit? What curriculum objectives will it fulfill?

1. **Library Media Standards:**
   Standard 1: The student who is information literate accesses information efficiently and effectively.
   Benchmark 1: Recognizes the need for information.
   Benchmark 2: Formulates questions based on information needs.

2. **Collaborative Content Standards:**
   Reading:
   Standard 1: The student reads and comprehends text across the curriculum.
   Benchmark 2: The student reads and comprehends text across the curriculum.
   Benchmark 3: The student expands vocabulary.

Level: First–Third grade reading   **Teacher's Name:**
Title: *"Let's Get a Pup!" Said Kate*
Time to Be Completed: Two 30-minute sessions

One-Sentence Summary of the Assignment: What is the student to do? (Step 1) What will he have to show for it? (Step 4)

Students will record and discuss story sequence and story details following the action of the main character in the story *"Let's Get a Pup!" Said Kate* by Bob Graham.

Finished Product Evaluation: What are the criteria and method by which the student will be graded? (Step 4)

• Student places the selected picture cards from the story on the Story Hand that correctly matches the steps of the Handy 3 Model.
• Student retells the sequences of the story using the picture cards while the teacher records the information dictated on the large Story Hand.

Plan of Action: What activities will be used to reach the assignment outcomes? What new information will need to be presented? (Step 2)

Library Media Specialist

a. Gather resource materials and create picture cards.
b. Read *"Let's Get a Pup!" Said Kate* to the students.
c. Teach/review Handy 3 steps using poster, story, and the picture cards.

Classroom Teacher

a. Assist with retelling, matching sequence cards with Handy 3 steps.
b. Write down student's dictation about the main characters' actions.

Notes about Doing the Job: How is the unit developing; is the plan working? (Step 3)

Students need prompting and probing questions from the LMS and classroom teacher to assist in the retelling of the story. Students love the process of retelling the story using pictures from the text.

Process Evaluation: How well did it go; what should be done differently next time? Documentation for student achievement, i.e., % of students reaching benchmark. (Step 5)

Make the picture reproductions large enough for the whole class to see the details of the story sequence. Work together as a group and ask probing questions so that each student understands the essential detail that is important to the story sequence. It might help to enlarge (on the copier) the picture cards selected to retell the story in order to focus the eye on the details of the picture. Using the large hand chart, place the cards on the steps that correspond to the Handy 3 model.

Student Assessment Measures: (Student product that assesses each step)
1. Assignment—Students will recognize and select the correct story card that shows the main character identifying the problem.
2. Plan of Action—
3. Doing the Job—Students will recognize and select the correct story card that shows the main character implementing a plan of action in order to solve the problem.
4. Product Evaluation—
5. Process Evaluation—Students will decide if the main character did a good job while solving the problem by showing approval or disapproval using a thumbs up or thumbs down voting process.

Materials/Resources: Include only special requirements.

"Let's Get a Pup!" Said Kate by Bob Graham, large Story Hand chart (may be illustrated on a dry-erase board) or Handy 3 primary graphic organizer, Handy 3 poster (displayed near the pictures from the story), picture sequence cards (selected pictures that will show the problem being identified, planned, and solved by the main character in the book)

Plan of Action: Individual Lesson

Objective: (For today's lesson. There can be as many or as few objectives as necessary to do a day's lesson.)
Students will practice story sequencing and the problem-solving process.

Introduction: (Engaging students in the learning.)
Have a volunteer from the local animal shelter introduce the process of pet adoption. Invite a Delta Society Pet Partner / R.E.A.D.® (Reading Education Assistance Dog) volunteer to talk to students about responsible pet ownership.

Activity 1: (Description of the way learning is to occur–may or may not be assessed at this time.)
Read the book *"Let's Get a Pup!" Said Kate* by Bob Graham Review the picture cards made from the book. Put the story cards in order.

Activity 2: (Description of the way learning is to occur–may or may not be assessed at this time.)
Use the Handy 3 graphic organizer/Handy 5 version of the Story Hand (depending on grade level or semester) to organize the steps of the problem-solving process.

Assessment: (May be done at a later date.)
The students will accurately retell the story using the Story Hand or Handy 3 graphic organizer.

Student Reflection: (How is this going to help me to do the assignment, what was new today, etc.)
The Handy 3 has been expanded and the Handy 5 has been introduced to second semester second grade students and reinforced with third grade students.

Teacher Reflection: (How well did the lesson go?)
Have both posters up on the wall (Handy 3 and Handy 5) in the classroom that supports both of the problem-solving models. It is important to introduce the Handy 5 to second semester second grade students as a readiness activity. It will help launch students who will begin to use the Handy 5 process in the third grade. Younger students using the Story Hand have been told about the other steps, but have not had their significance fully taught. They have also seen examples in the Library Media Center of the Handy 5 Story Hand.

Collaborative Planning Outline   **Grades One–Three—The Handy 3**

Standards Accomplished Addressed
Where does this assignment fit? What curriculum objectives will it fulfill?

1. **Library Media Standards:**
   Standard 1: The student who is information literate accesses information efficiently and effectively.
   Benchmark 1: Recognizes the need for information.
   Benchmark 3: Formulates questions based on informational needs.

2. **Collaborative Content Standards:**
   Counseling: Personal and Social Development
   Standard 2: Benchmark 1: The student will acquire self-knowledge and skills to make decisions and set goals.
   Standard 3: Benchmark 1: The student will acquire personal safety skills.

Level: First-third grade counseling   **Teacher's Name:**
Title: "Peanut's Emergency"
Time to Be Completed: Two 30-minute session for the LMS; one 40-minute session with the school counselor.

One-Sentence Summary of the Assignment: What is the student to do? (Step 1) What will he have to show for it? (Step 4)

The student will understand the options that several common emergencies contain and brainstorm about possible solutions and complete emergency cards and a Handy 3 student problem-solving handbook.

Finished Product Evaluation: What are the criteria and method by which the student will be graded? (Step 4)

- Student makes an emergency safe rule information card.
- Student illustrates the emergency and solution, using the Handy 3 student handbook.

Plan of Action: What activities will be used to reach the assignment outcomes? What new information will need to be presented? (Step 2)

Library Media Specialist

a. Read *Peanut's Emergency* and discuss possible solutions from the perspective of the main character.
b. Record the information on the Handy 3 graphic organizer.
c. Review information on the child safety website. Play a few games and discuss the other related activities.

Classroom Teacher

a. Complete the safety rules and emergency information cards.
b. Review the story *Peanut's Emergency* and have students draw their solutions on the Handy 3 handbook.

Notes about Doing the Job: How is the unit developing; is the plan working? (Step 3)

The counselor often teaches several grade level classes at one time, while the librarian teaches one class at a time. The librarian will have to start the lesson a week ahead of the counselor and make sure each student is ready for the session with the counselor.

Process Evaluation: How well did it go, what should be done differently next time? Documentation for student achievement, i.e., % of students reaching benchmark. (Step 5)

Students have asked many questions about finding and knowing emergency information. Students find the graphic organizer a helpful way to see events visually organized from the story. This made the completion of the Handy 3 student handbook emergency cards much easier to complete.

Student Assessment Measures: (Student product that assesses each step)
1. Assignment—Students will record solutions to several emergencies on the Handy 3 handbook.
2. Plan of Action—Students will complete emergency information/safety rules card.
3. Doing the Job—Review, discuss, and record possible solutions on either the graphic organizer or handbook.
4. Product Evaluation—Completed emergency card and parent review letter to take home and discuss with parents.
5. Process Evaluation—Students share with parents their personal safety and emergency information card statistics.

Materials/Resources: Include only special requirements.

Holyoke, Nancy. *Yikes A Smart Girl's Guide to Surviving Tricky, Sticky, Icky Situations.* Minneapolis, MN: Tandem Library, 2003.
Salat, Christina. *Peanut's Emergency.* Watertown, MA: Charlesbridge Pub., 2002.

URLs

Use www.mcgruff.org as a resource to present information about child safety. The site provides games, worksheets, activities, and cartoon clips to reinforce important issues. Download the emergency checklist, safety list and emergency information card from the publishers website at www.charlesbridge.com. Could reproduce the same information found on the back flap of the book.

Collaborative Planning Outline   **Kindergarten—Social Studies**

Standards Accomplished Addressed
Where does this assignment fit? What curriculum objectives will it fulfill?

1. **Library Media Standards:**
   Standard 1: The student who is information literate accesses information efficiently and effectively.
   Benchmark 3: Formulates questions based on information needs.

2. **Collaborative Content Standards:**
   Civics Government:
   2.2: The student knows the qualities of law-abiding citizens (e.g., honesty, courage, patriotism, respect.)

   Writing Standard:
   1.1.2: The student begins to orally communicate and/or write using personal experience (Ideas and Content; prewriting, drafting, revising.)

Level: Kindergarten social studies   **Teacher's Name:**
Title: "When I Was Brave…."
Time to Be Completed: Five 30-minute sessions

One-Sentence Summary of the Assignment: What is the student to do? (Step 1) What will he have to show for it? (Step 4)

The students will demonstrate their ability to compare their own life experiences to those heroes that they have been introduced to by writing stories using invented spelling, drawing, coloring, or pasting pictures, which will then be showcased on the class webpage.

Finished Product Evaluation: What are the criteria and method by which the student will be graded? (Step 4)

- Student interviews someone he or she considers a hero and relates the information to the rest of the class.
- Student demonstrates reflection on the information presented by comparing personal stories to those resulting from information presented by the instructor.
- Student chooses, identifies, or creates visual information to help relate the story and combine it with his or her own written product (which may be dictated to an adult) to produce a finished product.

Plan of Action: What activities will be used to reach the assignment outcomes? What new information will need to be presented? (Step 2)

Library Media Specialist	**Classroom Teacher**
a. Read stories about heroes, both adult and children.	a. Introduce the concept of heroes and discuss.
b. Help students brainstorm heroes to research.	b. Help students construct their stories, take dictation when necessary.
c. Help students create visual information to combine with their written product.	c. Demonstrate concept of comparison and model comparing personal story to own story.

Notes about Doing the Job: How is the unit developing, is the plan working? (Step 3)

Students seem to handle the steps okay.

Process Evaluation: How well did it go; what should be done differently next time? Documentation for student achievement, i.e., % of students reaching benchmark. (Step 5)

Student achievement will be based on completion of each step of the assignment. Each step of the process evaluation will be 10% of the student's grade.

Might use social bookmarking software such as *Del.ic.ious* to provide students the opportunity to explore sites such as Library of Congress's *American Memory*. Might provide the example that this unit is based on first so that students know what they are working toward. Might involve other school personnel in the project, such as the principal, janitor, paraprofessionals, and possibly community members such as policemen and firemen.

Student Assessment Measures: (Student product that assesses each step)
1. Assignment—Thumbs up–thumbs down to answer questions about assignment.
2. Plan of Action—Brainstorm list.
3. Doing the Job—Observation, students staying on task with minimal redirection from teachers.
4. Product Evaluation—Rubric, sharing stories.
5. Process Evaluation—Class discussion reflecting on each part of the assignment.

Materials/Resources: Include only special requirements.

Brave Irene by William Steig; *Shelia Ray, the Brave* by Kevin Henkes; *Brave Charlotte* by Anu Stohner; *Brave Norman: A True Story* by Andrew Clements

Adapted from comsewogue.k12.ny.us/%7Ecsinger/projects/braveirene/bravememories.htm (accessed 2 January 2006)

Collaborative Planning Outline   **Kindergarten—Science/Social Studies**

Standards Accomplished Addressed
Where does this assignment fit? What curriculum objectives will it fulfill?

1. **Library Media Standards:**
   Standard 1: The student who is information literate uses information efficiently and effectively.

2. **Collaborative Content Standards:**
   Science:
   Students will demonstrate the ability to distinguish between the four seasons.

Level: Kindergarten–science/social studies   **Teacher's Name:**
Title: "The Four Seasons"
Time to Be Completed: Five 30-minute sessions

One-Sentence Summary of the Assignment: What is the student to do? (Step 1) What will he have to show for it? (Step 4)

The student will research with a partner the four seasons, and then prepare a mini-book to share with class.

Finished Product Evaluation: What are the criteria and method by which the student will be graded? (Step 4)

- Student demonstrates completeness and quality of the graphic organizer.
- Student demonstrates completeness and accuracy of sentences for each season in the mini-book.
- Student demonstrates cooperation with partner at the research station.
- Student demonstrates quality answers on self-evaluation.

Plan of Action: What activities will be used to reach the assignment outcomes? What new information will need to be presented? (Step 2)

Library Media Specialist

a. Read fiction and non-fiction about the four seasons.
b. Help student locate resources.
c. Help students with research process.

Classroom Teacher

a. Introduce the concept of four seasons and discuss.
b. Demonstrate how to use the graphic organizer for information gathering.
c. Organize students into partner groups.
d. Monitor students as they work.

Notes about Doing the Job: How is the unit developing; is the plan working? (Step 3)

The plan is working well. Filling out the graphic organizer is time consuming but necessary in the research process.

Process Evaluation: How well did it go, what should be done differently next time? Documentation for student achievement, i.e., % of students reaching benchmark. (Step 5)

The project went well. More work and modeling needs to be done in the basic steps one goes through to collect the information. Students need to have more practice in filling out graphic organizers. Doing this project in the late spring would be helpful with this age because of difficulty with drawing and the mechanics involved in writing the sentences.

Student Assessment Measures: (Student product that assesses each step)
1. Assignment—Class discussion with thumbs up-thumbs down for understanding.
2. Plan of Action—Develop questions for graphic organizer.
3. Doing the Job—Fill out graphic organizer.
4. Product Evaluation—Presentation of mini-book about the seasons to the class.
5. Process Evaluation—Reflection paper with smiley faces to denote satisfaction levels.

Materials/Resources: Include only special requirements.

Collaborative Planning Outline   **Grade One—Science**

Standards Accomplished Addressed

Where does this assignment fit? What curriculum objectives will it fulfill?

1. **Library Media Standards:**
   Standard 3: Know about fiction and non-fiction books

2. **Collaborative Content Standards:**
   Science:
   3.1.1: Identify the parts of plants (roots, stem, leaves, and flower). (Introduce.)
   3.2.1: Compare characteristics of various plants (roots, stem, leaves, and flower). (Reinforce.)

Level: 1st grade—science   **Teacher's Name:**
Title: "Getting the Dirt on Plants"
Time to Be Completed: Library, four 20-minute sessions; Class, three times a week for 4 weeks, 30-minute sessions.

One-Sentence Summary of the Assignment: What is the student to do? (Step 1) What will he have to show for it? (Step 4)

After learning the differences between fiction and non-fiction books, students will create a Venn diagram comparing and contrasting the two types.

Finished Product Evaluation: What are the criteria and method by which the student will be graded? (Step 4)

•   Student lists at least three ideas in the right and left side of the Venn Diagram.
•   Student lists at least two ideas in the middle of the Venn Diagram.

Plan of Action: What activities will be used to reach the assignment outcomes? What new information will need to be presented? (Step 2)

Library Media Specialist

a. Introduce unit with teacher.
b. Read *Fran's Flower*, discuss characteristics of fiction books.
c. Read *Plants We Know*, discuss characteristics of non-fiction books.
d. Help students fill out Venn Diagram.

Classroom Teacher

a. Introduce unit with LMS.
b. Teach parts of a plant and how to label.
c. Teach characteristics and functions of each part of the plant.
d. Conduct assessment.

Notes about Doing the Job: How is the unit developing; is the plan working? (Step 3)

Check with students before checkout time each day to ask review questions about the difference between fiction and nonfiction books. Each day before student completes task, have a student or two repeat directions, and then have other students give a thumbs-up or thumbs-down. If students do not have enough time to complete each day's task, finish the next week. Use positive reinforcement to make sure students are staying on task.

Process Evaluation: How well did it go, what should be done differently next time? Documentation for student achievement, i.e., % of students reaching benchmark. (Step 5)

Next time, I would spend two weeks on each type of book and give more examples. I would also have students tell me what kinds of books they checked out each week as their "ticket" out the door. I do feel that my students understand the difference.

Student Assessment Measures: (Student product that assesses each step)
1. Assignment—Do a Think-Pair-Share* to check for understanding
2. Plan of Action—Discussion of characteristics of fiction and non-fiction
3. Doing the Job—Write 2–3 sentences for each type of book and fill out Venn Diagram.
4. Product Evaluation—Venn Diagram
5. Process Evaluation—Reflection on the process of filling out graphic organizer

Materials/Resources: Include only special requirements.

Fran's Flowers by Lisa Bruce, *Plants We Know (New True Books)* by Irene Miner, or any other primary level nonfiction book about plants, example of completed Venn diagram, blank Venn Diagram

*Think-pair-share—The teacher asks an open-ended question and gives students a half to one minute to think about the question. Students then pair with up and discuss their thoughts about the question for several minutes. The teacher then asks for discussion or works for consensus among the class members.

Collaborative Planning Outline   **Grade One—Art**

Standards Accomplished Addressed
Where does this assignment fit? What curriculum objectives will it fulfill?

1. **Library Media Standards:**
   Standard 2: The student who is information literate evaluates information critically and competently.
   Benchmark 2: Distinguishes between fiction, point of view, and opinion.

   Standard 3: The student who is information literate uses information accurately and creatively.
   Benchmark 4: Produces and communicates information and ideas in appropriate Formats.

2. **Collaborative Content Standards:**
   Art:
   Standard 1: Understanding and applying media, techniques, and processes.
   Benchmark: By the end of 2nd grade, students will be able to explore the use of media, techniques, and processes.

   Standard 2: Using knowledge of structures and functions.
   Benchmark 4: By the end of 2nd grade, students will be able to recognize differences among visual characteristics and purposes of art.

Level: 1st-grade art   **Teacher's Name:**
Title: "My Colorful Neighborhood"
Time to Be Completed: Four 30-minute sessions.

One-Sentence Summary of the Assignment: What is the student to do? (Step 1) What will he have to show for it? (Step 4)

The student will demonstrate understanding of the concept of neighborhoods and primary and secondary colors by creating a painting of his/her neighborhood using only one secondary color.

Finished Product Evaluation: What are the criteria and method by which the student will be graded? (Step 4)

• Painting depicts a view of student's neighborhood with which he/she is familiar (his/her point of view).
• Student successfully mixes primary colors to create a secondary color.
• Painting uses only one secondary color.
• Student uses materials safely and appropriately.

Plan of Action: What activities will be used to reach the assignment outcomes? What new information will need to be presented? (Step 2)

<u>**Library Media Specialist**</u>

a. Read *Harold and the Purple Crayon* to class.
b. Discuss characteristics of neighborhoods.
c. Show pictures of different types of neighborhoods from books and magazines.

<u>**Classroom Teacher**</u>

a. Introduce the color wheel.
b. Discuss primary and secondary colors.
c. Explain or demonstrate paint mixing procedures and appropriate use of tools and materials.

Notes about Doing the Job: How is the unit developing; is the plan working? (Step 3)

Are students attentive when the story is read in class? Do they respond to questions and discuss how their neighborhoods are different and what makes each one special? Is there enough time for cutting out pictographs for the graphic organizer or should they be cut ahead of time? Are students engaged using pictographs or should they look for pictures in old magazines to use on the graphic organizer? Is there enough time for the art portion of the lesson? Are students on task in the art room?

Process Evaluation: How well did it go; what should be done differently next time? Documentation for student achievement, i.e., % of students reaching benchmark. (Step 5)

This lesson is for very early in the school year, but if used later in the year, students could write sentences to show understanding of the assignment and for process evaluation. Add Think-Pair-Share after reading and discussion, but before painting the picture to emphasize individual points of view. The assignment is simple, but provides a good introduction to follow-up lesson on maps and map reading.

Student Assessment Measures: (Student product that assesses each step)
1. Assignment—Thumbs up-thumbs down for understanding.
2. Plan of Action—Graphic organizer.
3. Doing the Job—Teacher observation of students.
4. Product Evaluation—Rubric.
5. Process Evaluation—Class brainstorm: What did students like, not like, do differently next time?

Materials/Resources: Include only special requirements.

Harold and the Purple Crayon by Crockett Johnson, books and magazines with neighborhood pictures, color wheels, primary tempera paint

Adapted from artsedge.kennedy-center.org/content/2373/ (accessed 2 January 2006)

Collaborative Planning Outline   **Grade Two—Science**

Standards Accomplished Addressed
Where does this assignment fit? What curriculum objectives will it fulfill?

1. **Library Media Standards:**
    Standard 3: The student who is information literate uses information accurately and creatively.
    Benchmark 1: Organizes information for practical application.

2. **Collaborative Content Standards:**
    Life Science:
    Standard 3: As a result of the activities for grades K–2, all students will begin to develop an understanding of biological concepts.
    Benchmark 3: All students will develop an understanding of the characteristics of living things. Through direct experiences, students will observe living things, their life cycles, and their habitats.

Level: 2nd-grade science   **Teacher's Name:**
Title: "Life Cycles"
Time to Be Completed: Twenty 20-minute sessions

One-Sentence Summary of the Assignment: What is the student to do? (Step 1) What will he have to show for it? (Step 4)

Working with a partner, students will research the life cycle of an animal and prepare a model or poster with fact cards.

Finished Product Evaluation: What are the criteria and method by which the student will be graded? (Step 4)

*   Student completes the graphic organizers with quality information.
*   The model or poster reflects an accurate life cycle of the animal or insect.
*   The model or poster is appealing and sequential.
*   The facts are correct and neatly written.
*   Partners work together in a cooperative way.

Rubrics

4—All aspects of the life cycle project were complete and accurate.
3—Most of the elements of the life cycle project were complete and accurate.
2—Only part of the project reflected an understanding of the animal's life cycle.
1—There were serious misunderstandings of the life cycle project.

Plan of Action: What activities will be used to reach the assignment outcomes? What new information will need to be presented? (Step 2)

Library Media Specialist

a. Gather books on animal life cycles.
b. Locate Internet sites to be used.
c. Provide videos on animals.
d. Teach note-taking process.
e. Read related books during library time.
f. Show plastic models of the butterfly and frog life cycles.

Classroom Teacher

a. Introduce life cycle concept with live butterfly eggs and a tadpole in the classroom.
b. Read books and show videos.
c. Explain graphic organizers.
d. Organize working pairs.
e. Help students develop individual questions for fact cards.
f. Oversee and evaluate the research and projects.

Notes about Doing the Job: How is the unit developing; is the plan working? (Step 3)

Students had a hard time developing questions. Need a few more resources at a lower reading level.

Process Evaluation: How well did it go; what should be done differently next time? Documentation for student achievement, i.e., % of students reaching benchmark. (Step 5)

Do more introductory work on life cycles in general so students have some background to begin developing questions. Perhaps using a KWL chart would be useful.

Student Assessment Measures: (Student product that assesses each step)
1. Assignment—Write a list of assignment criteria.
2. Plan of Action—Partners develop questions to guide research.
3. Doing the Job—Teacher observation of group work, making note card, preparation of poster/model.
4. Product Evaluation—Rubric.
5. Process Evaluation—Student reflection on teamwork and self.

Materials/Resources: Include only special requirements.

Nonfiction books on life cycles
Life Cycle of a Frog–Big Book by Angela Royston, *The Life Cycle of a Frog* (with audio CD); *Early Theme: Life Cycles: Butterflies, Chicks, Frogs, and More* by Marcia Land; *I Wonder Why Caterpillars Eat So Much and Other Questions about Life Cycles* by Belinda Weber; *From Caterpillar to Butterfly* by Deborah Heiligman

Videos on life cycles

Internet Resources
Google: Frog Life Cycles: Images, Google: Butterfly Life Cycles, "Children's Butterfly Site." July 2006; bsi.montana.edu/web/kidsbutterfly/"Frog Life Cycle." July 2006.
ecs.lewisham.gov.uk/youthspace/cu/Lorraing/growth_info_of_butterly.htm

Collaborative Planning Outline   **Grade Two—Science**

Standards Accomplished Addressed
Where does this assignment fit? What curriculum objectives will it fulfill?

1. **Library Media Standards:**
   Standard 1: The student who is information literate uses information efficiently and effectively.

2. **Collaborative Content Standards:**
   Science:
   The student will observe, investigate, and compare how living organisms interact with one another and their environment.

Level: 2nd-grade science   **Teacher's Name:**
Title: "Creatures of the Deep"
Time to Be Completed: Ten 30-minute sessions

One-Sentence Summary of the Assignment: What is the student to do? (Step 1) What will he have to show for it? (Step 4)

Students will research a specific ocean animal, write a 1–2 page report, and illustrate it with a drawing of the animal.

Finished Product Evaluation: What are the criteria and method by which the student will be graded? (Step 4)

- Report is 1–2 neatly written pages.
- Report uses at least two sources, one being the CD-ROM encyclopedia.
- Report is stapled onto large sheet of construction paper with an illustration of the ocean animal drawn by the student on the remaining half.

Plan of Action: What activities will be used to reach the assignment outcomes? What new information will need to be presented? (Step 2)

Library Media Specialist

a. Take the questions discussed in class and make a graphic organizer.
b. Model how to use the index, table of contents, and key words.
c. Introduce how to use the CD-ROM and key word search.
d. Introduce how to cite sources.

Classroom Teacher

a. Introduce the ocean and animals that live there.
b. Have students choose animal to learn about.
c. Provide opportunity to use the resources to fill in graphic organizer.
d. Observe students' progress.
e. Display finished reports in hallway.

Notes about Doing the Job: How is the unit developing; is the plan working? (Step 3)

Students enjoyed learning to use the CD-ROM. Break small groups down into smaller groups for beginning instruction on key word searching. Need to work with students a little more on proper way to do peer editing.

Process Evaluation: How well did it go; what should be done differently next time? Documentation for student achievement, i.e., % of students reaching benchmark. (Step 5)

Students found graphic organizer easy to use. Modeling was essential at this stage to introduce concepts. It was a successful unit and would like to do a similar one again. Teacher and LMS working in collaboration to keep students up to speed and on task.

Student Assessment Measures: (Student product that assesses each step)
1. Assignment—Thumbs up-thumbs down to check for understanding
2. Plan of Action—Graphic organizer
3. Doing the Job—Notes on proper section of graphic organizer, use of index and CD-ROM, rough draft, editing notes
4. Product Evaluation—Illustrated report, rubric
5. Process Evaluation—Student and teacher conference

Materials/Resources: Include only special requirements.

Graphic organizer, writing paper, blue construction paper, nonfiction books on ocean animals, CD-ROM encyclopedia

Collaborative Planning Outline   **Grade Three—Science**

Standards Accomplished Addressed
Where does this assignment fit? What curriculum objectives will it fulfill?

1. **Library Media Standards:**
   Standard 3: The student who is information literature uses information accurately and creatively.

2. **Collaborative Content Standards:**
   Science:
   Students will understand the components and characteristics of various plants and animal habitats and be able to apply scientific knowledge for a variety of purposes.

Level: 3rd-grade science
Title: "Animal Habitats"   **Teacher's Name:**
Time to Be Completed: Ten 30-minute sessions

One-Sentence Summary of the Assignment: What is the student to do? (Step 1) What will he have to show for it? (Step 4)

Students will research, design, and create habitat diorama with written explanation, a paragraph about a food web, and a poem about how we can help the environment.

Finished Product Evaluation: What are the criteria and method by which the student will be graded? (Step 4)

- Habitat labels include characteristics, components, plants and animals
- Four-line rhyming poem about helping our environment has a title and is computer generated
- Food web paragraph, contains an introduction, three detailed sentences, and a conclusion
- All work includes quality, neatness and organization, appropriate word choice, follows directions, and completes work on time

Plan of Action: What activities will be used to reach the assignment outcomes? What new information will need to be presented? (Step 2)

<u>Library Media Specialist</u>

a. Introduce electronic encyclopedias
b. Introduce content area CD-ROMs
c. Develop search strategy
d. Monitor research time in LMC

<u>Classroom Teacher</u>

a. Introduce guide for planning the project
b. Review assignment
c. Present content material
d. Provide time for journal writing and cooperative groups

Notes about Doing the Job: How is the unit developing; is the plan working? (Step 3)

Structured journal writing, students working in pairs to write questions for statements in text, chapter tests, graphic organizers about food chains, guided practice in drawing food webs, co-operative groups to develop written paragraphs, simulation and brainstorming about scavengers and decomposers

Process Evaluation: How well did it go; what should be done differently next time? Documentation for student achievement, i.e., % of students reaching benchmark. (Step 5)

Sufficient materials available. Timelines could be extended. Continue to stress quality work.

Student Assessment Measures: (Student product that assesses each step)
1. Assignment—Handprint of planning guide, thumbs up-thumbs down to indicate understanding
2. Plan of Action—Students develop own timelines to plan completion of projects
3. Doing the Job—Check timeline for progress
4. Product Evaluation—Students present their exhibits, teacher shares poems with class
5. Process Evaluation—Five-point rubric for each component assessed by teacher, student-written reflections on how they feel they did on the project. (See form next page.)

Materials/Resources: Include only special requirements.

CD-ROM Encyclopedia, *National Geographic Mammals*

Scoring Rubric for Finished Product
# indicates points given for each component
Grading Scale: A = 23-25; B = 20-22; C = 16-19; D = 14-15; F = 0-13

1. Competency Test	1	2	3	4	5
Chapter 11					
Chapter 12					
2. Diorama	1	2	3	4	5
Labeled food, space, shelter, water					
3. Four-Line Poem	1	2	3	4	5
Rhyming words					
Word processing					
4. Food Web Paragraph	1	2	3	4	5
Five sentences					
Organization					
Word processing					
5. Quality work	1	2	3	4	5
Neatly done					
Worked independently					
Completed on time					

3rd Grade - Animal Habitat Unit
Evaluation Checklist and Reflection

	Yes	No
Did my plan work?	_____	_____
Did I do my best work?	_____	_____

I am really proud of my diorama because:

Other people (parents, peers, or teachers) said my project was:

Collaborative Planning Outline   **Grade Three—Music**

Standards Accomplished Addressed
Where does this assignment fit? What curriculum objectives will it fulfill?

1. **Library Media Standards:**
   Standard 5: The student who is an independent learner is information literate and
   appreciates literature and other creative expressions of information.
   Benchmark 2: Derives meaning from information presented creatively in a
   variety of formats.

   Standard 7: The student who contributes positively to the learning community
   and to society is information literate and recognizes the importance of information
   to a democratic society.
   Benchmark 1: Seeks information from diverse sources, contexts, disciplines,
   and cultures.

2. **Collaborative Content Standards:**
   Music:
   Content Standard 6: Listening to, analyzing, and describing music.
   Achievement Standard: Students demonstrate perceptual skills by moving, by
   answering questions about, and describing examples of music of various styles
   representing diverse cultures.

   Content Standard 9: Understanding music in relation to history and culture.
   Achievement Standard: Students identify by genre or style aural examples of
   music from various historical periods and cultures.

Level: 3rd-grade music   **Teacher's Name:**
Title: "A Meeting of Jazz and Poetry"
Time to Be Completed: Three one-hour sessions

One-Sentence Summary of the Assignment: What is the student to do? (Step 1) What will he have to
show for it? (Step 4)

Students will create and present a two-stanza poem (two quatrains) at a simulated Poetry Café
after reviewing various jazz and poetry resources.

Finished Product Evaluation: What are the criteria and method by which the student will be graded? (Step
4)

- Poem is written with two stanzas in a quatrain format of ABAB.
- Poem is a blues topic "what gets you down" but remains appropriate.
- Poem is presented at Poetry Café session.
- Oral presentation stresses eye contact, voice, and posture during presentation.
- Rubric criteria are met separately for poem and presentation.

Plan of Action: What activities will be used to reach the assignment outcomes? What new information will need to be presented? (Step 2)

Library Media Specialist

a. Make available resources about Louisiana jazz, jazz musicians, and jazz poetry.
b. Introduce students to various poets who have had an influence in jazz music—focus on Langston Hughes.
c. Read jazz poetry and lyrics.
d. Demonstrate how common poetry, such as Mother Goose, has been used in jazz music—listen to jazz CD.

Classroom Teacher

a. Play jazz music and have students evaluate the elements of jazz.
b. Discuss history and culture of jazz in Louisiana.
c. Highlight famous jazz musicians from our state.
d. Create a jazz and Poetry Café setting for the presentation of the poems at the last class meeting for the unit.

Notes about Doing the Job: How is the unit developing; is the plan working? (Step 3)

Watch for students' reactions, time constraints, and age-appropriateness the first time with this unit.

Process Evaluation: How well did it go; what should be done differently next time? Documentation for student achievement, i.e., % of students reaching benchmark. (Step 5)

Check that the unit activities actually meet the identified standards and that the collaboration and integration of the subject matter worked well.

Student Assessment Measures: (Student product that assesses each step)
1. Assignment—Class discussion of assignment elements to check that all students understand.
2. Plan of Action—Student reviews various jazz poetry and listens to music and lyrics to get creative ideas.
3. Doing the Job—Teacher observation of student work during three days of writing.
4. Product Evaluation—Students present their poems at the Poetry Café. Rubric used to score work.
5. Process Evaluation—One-on-one conference with LMS and music teacher.

Materials/Resources: Include only special requirements.

Non-fiction books about jazz in Louisiana, jazz musicians and poets, variety of jazz CDs, decorations to create Poetry Café, food for Poetry Café (cheese, crackers, apple juice)

Collaborative Planning Outline   **Grade Three–Five—Language Arts**

Standards Accomplished Addressed
Where does this assignment fit? What curriculum objectives will it fulfill?

1. **Library Media Standards:**
   Standard 7: The student who contributes positively to the learning community and to society is information literate and recognizes the importance of information to a democratic society.
   Benchmark 2: Respects the principle of equitable access to information.

2. **Collaborative Content Standards:**
   Language Arts:
   Standard 1: Students read a wide range of print and non-print texts to build an understanding of texts, of themselves, and of the culture of the United States and the world; to acquire new information; to respond to the needs and demands of society and the workplace; and for personal fulfillment. Among these texts are fiction and non-fiction, classic, and contemporary works.

   Standard 2: Students read a wide range of literature from many periods in many genres to build understanding of the many dimensions (e.g., philosophical, ethical, aesthetic) of the human experience.

Level: 3rd–5th-grade language arts   **Teacher's Name:**
Title: "A Case for Reading—Examining Challenged and Banned Books"
Time to Be Completed: Five 50-minute sessions

One-Sentence Summary of the Assignment: What is the student to do? (Step 1) What will he have to show for it? (Step 4)

The student, with a partner, will examine the issue of censorship by choosing and reading a grade-appropriate banned or challenged book, and will critically evaluate the book by developing and supporting a position as to what should be done with that book in the school library by writing a persuasive essay to share with the class.

Finished Product Evaluation: What are the criteria and method by which the student will be graded? (Step 4)

Student demonstrates an understanding of the issue of censorship by his or her examination of the content of the chosen book.
- Creativity and originality of ideas
- Persuasiveness of the essay
- Presentation of the essay
- Grammar and spelling
- Capitalization and punctuation

Plan of Action: What activities will be used to reach the assignment outcomes? What new information will need to be presented? (Step 2)

Library Media Specialist

a. Send a letter home to the parents to explain the activity.
b. Make a display of banned or challenged books to use in the classroom.
c. Make a list of age-appropriate banned or challenged books for the students to choose to read.
d. Copy the ALA definition of censorship and information on Banned Book Week.
e. Bookmark websites that explore the issue of censorship.
f. Makes copies of persuasion map for the class. Demonstrate its use with the teacher.

Classroom Teacher

a. Discuss the issue of censorship with the class. Give examples.
b. Share the ALA definition of censorship. Discuss books that have been banned or challenge and have students give their views.
c. Have students, working in pairs, choose a book to read. Make use of the websites.
d. Provide time for students to take notes on reasons for challenge and to form an opinion on what should be done with the book in the school library.
e. Provide time to prepare a persuasive essay to share with the class.
f. Explain grading rubric and criteria for grading.

Notes about Doing the Job: How is the unit developing; is the plan working? (Step 3)

Brainstorming with the entire class for the first assignment period worked well. They all verbally stated that they understood the assignment. Also, working in pairs and sharing ideas for the next three assignment periods was successful. Check persuasive maps after second-class period to make sure students are on the right track.

Process Evaluation: How well did it go; what should be done differently next time? Documentation for student achievement, i.e., % of students reaching benchmark. (Step 5)

The persuasive essays/presentations created stimulating discussion on the issue of censorship. The graphic organizers were particularly helpful for students to gather their thoughts and make their persuasive arguments for their essays. However, more time is needed to complete assignment—at least one more time period.

Student Assessment Measures: (Student product that assesses each step)
 1. Assignment—List the specific criteria for the assignment.
 2. Plan of Action—Fill out graphic organizer.
 3. Doing the Job—Write persuasive essay and present to the class.
 4. Product Evaluation—Rubric reassuring the six elements of the assignment.
 5. Process Evaluation—Brainstorm with class on what they learned from the essays.

Materials/Resources: Include only special requirements.

Letter to parents, a list and selected banned and challenged books, appropriate reference materials on censorship, persuasive map organizer

Adapted from www.readwritethink.org

Collaborative Planning Outline   **Grade Four—Language Arts**

Standards Accomplished Addressed
Where does this assignment fit? What curriculum objectives will it fulfill?

1. **Library Media Standards:**
   Standard 2: The student who is information literate evaluates information critically and competently.
   Benchmark 1: The student determines accuracy, relevance, and comprehensiveness.
   Benchmark 2: The student distinguishes among fact, point of view, and opinion.

2. **Collaborative Content Standards:**
   Language Arts
   Standard 1.2.2: The student writes for a variety of audiences, purposes, and contexts.

   Standard 1.2.14: The student writes expository texts using the writing process. The student chooses words and phrases appropriate for purposes and audience.

Level: 4th–grade language arts   **Teacher's Name:**
Title: "The Lansing Intermediate Daily Post: Creating a Classroom Newspaper"
Time to Be Completed: Fifteen 45–60-minute sessions

One-Sentence Summary of the Assignment: What is the student to do? (Step 1) What will he have to show for it? (Step 4)

Students will organize facts to compose newspaper articles describing important events occurring at Lansing Intermediate School.

Finished Product Evaluation: What are the criteria and method by which the student will be graded? (Step 4)

- Completes at least a single paragraph newspaper article about an event occurring in and/or around Lansing Intermediate School during the current school year, including a title, a lead, the 5 Ws (Who, What, When, Where, Why,) and four additional details, listing them from greatest to least importance to the overall story.
- Creates meaningful illustrations that add to and coordinate with written information.
- Uses facts as opposed to opinions within the article's content.
- Works well with group members to create, edit, and publish the newspaper article.
- General expectations of quality work, neat and organized, follows directions, and completes work on time.

Plan of Action: What activities will be used to reach the assignment outcomes? What new information will need to be presented? (Step 2)

Library Media Specialist

a. Introduce newspapers to students.
b. Read *Fairytale News* and empha- size the characteristics of a news- paper article.
c. Review parts of a newspaper arti- cle, discuss importance of using facts rather than opinions.
d. Use graphic organizer to diagram parts of a newspaper story.
e. Discuss format of newspaper, sec- tions, and articles.
f. Discuss interviewing techniques.
g. Demonstrate using note cards to record questions to be asked.
h. Compose letter to teachers con- cerning project their students are working on.
i. Review newspaper layout, review online and paper copies before students begin final draft.

Classroom Teacher

a. Check for prior knowledge.
b. Examine real-world newspapers to identify different sections.
c. Use nursery rhymes to introduce the 5 Ws of a newspaper article.
d. Read *The Furry News: How to Make a Newspaper* and review the sections.
e. Brainstorm the article types stu- dents can write about and group these articles into categories or sections.
f. Group students, based on inter- est, into newspaper sections.
g. Check graphic organizers before students begin drafts.
h. Provide class time for students to self-evaluate their drafts.
i. Provide time to work on final draft using computer lab.
j. Print copies for each student and provide time for them to enjoy.
k. Present a copy to the school prin- cipal.
l. Assess product and process using rubrics.

Notes about Doing the Job: How is the unit developing; is the plan working? (Step 3)

Check for scheduling issues, student understanding of assignment and its objectives, adequate knowledge base prior, and amount of on-task behavior.

Process Evaluation: How well did it go; what should be done differently next time? Documentation for student achievement, i.e., % of students reaching benchmark. (Step 5)

Is the independent nature of the project too overwhelming for students? Was there enough time to adequately complete the instruction and the product? Was the assignment defined clearly? Were the objectives met successfully, or do they need to be modified?

Student Assessment Measures: (Student product that assesses each step)
1. Assignment—Thumbs up-thumbs down to check for understanding
2. Plan of Action—Graphic organizer and interview questions
3. Doing the Job—Draft of newspaper article
4. Product Evaluation—Rubric for article and group work
5. Process Evaluation—Student project evaluation checklist and reflection on process

Materials/Resources: Include only special requirements.

Books included in bibliography, writing textbook, colored pencils, crayons, or markers, access to computer lab, digital camera and/or scanner (if available), relevant websites included in bibliography

Adapted from www.readwritethink.org

Bibliography:

Brooks, W. R. *Freddy and the Bean Home News.* New York: Puffin, 2002.

Burns' Bunch Website (www.brookfield.k12.mo.us/Elementary/Burns/february1.html)

Class 4D's Website (www.geocities.com/mirmt1/pproj.html)

The Educator's Reference Desk Lesson Plans Website
   (www.eduref.org/cgi-bin/printlessons.cgi/Virtual/Lessons/Interdisciplinary/INT0051.html)

The Fourth Grade Times (tsweb.home.insightbb.com/news/planet.htm)

Gibbons, Gail. *Deadline! From News to Newspaper.* New York: HarperCollins, 1987.

Internet Public Library Website (www.ipl.org/div/news/)

Leedy, Loreen. *The Furry News: How to Make a Newspaper.* New York: Holiday House, 1990.

Mrs. Davie's Class Newspaper Website (www.fvrcs.gov.bc.ca/davies/news1.html)

Scoring Rubric for Finished Product

# indicates points given for each component

Grading Scale: A = 18-20; B = 16-17; C = 14-15; D = 12-13; F = 0-11

	1	2	3	4
1. Single Paragraph Newspaper Article	1	2	3	4
At least five sentences				
Organization (Introduction, details, and conclusion)				
Required Elements (Title, lead, 5 Ws, and 4 details)				
2. Facts	1	2	3	4
Uses facts versus opinions when reporting information				
3. Illustrations	1	2	3	4
Meaningful to the text				
Neat				
4. Group Work	1	2	3	4
Cooperative				
Listens well to others				
Actively participates in all group activities				
5. Quality Work	1	2	3	4
Neatly done				
Follows directions				
Completed on time				

TOTAL POINTS

Fourth Grade – Classroom Newspaper Project
Rubric Scoring

4   All criteria are met exceptionally well.

3   All criteria are met satisfactorily. **OR**

      Most criteria are met, some exceptionally well.

2   Many criteria are not met. There are major omissions or errors.

1   Few criteria are met. Submissions are unsatisfactory.

Fourth Grade – Classroom Newspaper Project

Student Evaluation Checklist and Reflection

	Yes	No
Did I complete the entire assignment?	_____	_____
Did I do my best work?	_____	_____

I am really proud of my biography because:

_____

_____

_____

_____

_____

_____

_____

_____

Other people (parents, peers, or teachers) said my project was:

_____

_____

_____

_____

_____

_____

_____

Collaborative Planning Outline   **Grade Four—Social Studies**

Standards Accomplished Addressed
Where does this assignment fit? What curriculum objectives will it fulfill?

1. **Library Media Standards:**
   Standard 2: The student who is information literate evaluates information critically and competently.
   Benchmark 2: Distinguishes between fact, point of view, and opinion.

   Standard 3: The student who is information literate uses information accurately and creatively.
   Benchmark 2: Integrate new information into one's own knowledge.

2. **Collaborative Content Standards:**
   History Standard:
   The student uses a working knowledge and understanding of significant individuals, groups, ideas, events, eras, and developments in the history of Kansas, the United States, and the world, utilizing essential analytical and research skills.
   Benchmark 2: The student understands the importance of experiences of groups of people who have contributed to the richness of heritage.

Level: 4th-grade social studies   **Teacher's Name:**
Title: "Lighting the Way to Freedom: What Would You Do as a Slave?"
Time to Be Completed: Twenty 30-minute sessions, ten sessions in the library

One-Sentence Summary of the Assignment: What is the student to do? (Step 1) What will he have to show for it? (Step 4)

After seeing the video *The Drinking Gourd* and discussing its implications, students, working in groups, will create a "freedom quilt" that reflects the hardships of slavery.

Finished Product Evaluation: What are the criteria and method by which the student will be graded? (Step 4)

- Student uses at least three "freedom symbols" on his or her quilt block.
- Student cooperates to complete a group quilt block that will consist of three or four squares that measure 6x6 inches.
- Student presents his or her finished quilt block to the class and explains the route used on the quilt block map.

Plan of Action: What activities will be used to reach the assignment outcomes? What new information will need to be presented? (Step 2)

Library Media Specialist

a. Check for prior knowledge about the Civil War.
b. Give the Underground Railroad pre-quiz.
c. Bookmark the Library of Congress website, National Geographic website.
d. Do a chart on the North and South as to why slaves were kept, reasons why they should be free.
e. Read *Sweet Clara and the Freedom Quilt.*
f. Lead discussion about *Sweet Clara* and reasons for traveling on the Underground Railroad and what symbols were used on quilts.
g. Help students access resources to discover additional symbols.

Classroom Teacher

a. Introduce the Civil War and Underground Railroad.
b. Talk about the concept of slavery.
c. Discuss free vs. slave states and slave routes.
d. Oversee the plantation drawing.
e. Show *Follow the Drinking Gourd.*
f. Provide time to work on quilt blocks, prepare materials, practice presentations.
g. Arrange to have quilt made.
h. Give Underground Railroad post-quiz.
i. Arrange for students to present "slave" narratives.

Notes about Doing the Job: How is the unit developing; is the plan working? (Step 3)

Are we (teacher and the LMS) providing enough information to the students? Are the students engaged in the website? Are they retaining the vocabulary? Are we giving them too much information too quickly?

Process Evaluation: How well did it go; what should be done differently next time? Documentation for student achievement, i.e., % of students reaching benchmark. (Step 5)

The students were very interested in this topic and the flow of the material seemed to be at the right pace for them. I think bringing over the laptops from the classroom and having students go to the National Geographic site themselves would work better next time.

Student Assessment Measures: (Student product that assesses each step)
1. Assignment—Class discussion to check for understanding of assignment.
2. Plan of Action—Graphic organizers for vocabulary and symbols.
3. Doing the Job—Observation of class work on group quilt blocks.
4. Product Evaluation—Rubric for quilt symbols, group work, and finished product.
5. Process Evaluation—Student survey.

Materials/Resources: Include only special requirements.

Books included in the bibliography, white paper, overhead, quiz, copy of free and slave states map, material cut to 6"x6" squares, cloth markers, scan-it converter to put websites on TV so the whole class can see

Bibliography:

Connelly, Bernadine. *Follow the Drinking Gourd*. New York: Scholastic, 1997.

Hopkinson, Deborah. *Sweet Clara and the Freedom Quilt*. New York: Knopf, 1993.

Levine, Ellen. *If You Traveled on The Underground Railroad*. New York: Scholastic, 1988.

Ringgold, Faith. *Aunt Harriet's Underground Railroad in the Sky*. New York: Crown, 1992.

URLs used:

Library of Congress. "African American History Website." n.d. at memory.loc.gov/ammem/browse/ListSome.php?category=African%20American%20History.

National Geographic. "History of Slavery." n.d. at www.nationalgeographic.com/railroad/j1.html. (accessed 13 July 2005).

Freedom Quilt

Name: _____   Teacher: _____

Date: _____   Title of Work: _____

	Criteria				Points
	1	**2**	**3**	**4**	
Quilt square	Did not complete square or poor quality	Completed square but only have 1 symbol and poorly completed	Square is neatly completed and has 2-3 symbols	Square is neatly completed, has 3-4 symbols and fits together in a theme	____
Working together to complete quilt square	Group did not work well together, teacher needed to intervene	A few arguments but worked them out on their own and worked together to complete task	1-2 arguments worked out and completed task	Worked together great and completed task without argument	____
Presented quilt block to the class	Did not explain symbols, could not be heard, no eye contact, only one person spoke from group	Showed quilt, explained part of quilt, only two people spoke	Explained and showed quilt, hard to hear, little eye contact	Explained loudly and clearly with everyone taking a turn to speak and good eye contact	____
					____
					____
				Total---->	____

Teacher Comments:

Powered by TeAch-nology.com- The Web Portal For Educators! (www.teach-nology.com)

Survey for process evaluation

1. The thing I liked the most about this unit was...
2. One thing I might change about this unit is…
3. An idea I have to add to this unit is…
4. How did you feel about working in both the library and the classroom?
5. What are two new things that you learned from this unit?

Collaborative Planning Outline   **Grade Five—Language Arts**

Standards Accomplished Addressed
Where does this assignment fit? What curriculum objectives will it fulfill?

1. **Library Media Standards:**
   Standard 1: The student who is information literate uses information efficiently and effectively.

   Standard 3: The student who is information literate uses information accurately and creatively.

2. **Collaborative Content Standards:**
   Language Arts:
   Students will demonstrate knowledge of literature from a variety of cultures, genres, and time periods.

Level: 5th-grade language arts   **Teacher's Name:**
Title: "A Slice of Life"
Time to Be Completed: Ten 30-minute sessions plus outside reading time

One-Sentence Summary of the Assignment: What is the student to do? (Step 1) What will he have to show for it? (Step 4)

Student will read a biography of their choice, formulate questions, and find answer to those questions, and share the information with a slice of life pizza report.

Finished Product Evaluation: What are the criteria and method by which the student will be graded? (Step 4)
- Student creates a pizza that contains eight questions and answers about the biographee.
- Student writes information neatly on each pizza slice.
- Student chooses name for pizza company that reflects a major event in the biographee's life.

Plan of Action: What activities will be used to reach the assignment outcomes? What new information will need to be presented? (Step 2)

Library Media Specialist

a. Introduce the biography genre
b. Help student formulate questions and develop graphic organizer
c. Set up pizza restaurant for students to share their reports
d. Arrange to have dessert pizza to share

Classroom Teacher

a. Introduce the project
b. Allow some class time for student reading
c. Help students design their pizza and write information on slices

Notes about Doing the Job: How is the unit developing; is the plan working? (Step 3)

Students had a difficult time locating biographies about people they were interested in. Haven't had much exposure to biographies, so they were unsure about what kinds of questions to formulate. Seemed to enjoy locating information to answer questions.

Process Evaluation: How well did it go; what should be done differently next time? Documentation for student achievement, i.e., % of students reaching benchmark. (Step 5)

Teacher and LMS evaluated together which was interesting. Need to purchase more biographies with a shorter, similar format to help make the work easier for students and teachers. Look at the Adler series (*A Picture Book of …*). Students enjoyed making and sharing the pizzas. See if school cooks (or parents) could make the dessert pizzas next year—it got too expensive to buy them.

Student Assessment Measures: (Student product that assesses each step)
1. Assignment—Section one of assignment planner.
2. Plan of Action—List of questions developed.
3. Doing the Job—Data chart with questions, answers, and resources used.
4. Product Evaluation—An eight-slice pizza.
5. Process Evaluation—Section five of the assignment planner.

Materials/Resources: Include only special requirements.

Medium pizza box and paper circles to fit box for each student, a model pizza to share, assignment planner, a data chart

Collaborative Planning Outline   **Grade Five—Language Arts/Social Studies**

Standards Accomplished Addressed
Where does this assignment fit? What curriculum objectives will it fulfill?

1. **Library Media Standards:**
   Standard 2: The student who is information literate evaluates information critically and competently.
   Benchmark 1: The student seeks multiple sources to verify accuracy of information.

   Standard 3: The student who is information literate uses information accurately and creatively.
   Benchmark 1: The student organizes an information product.

2. **Collaborative Content Standards:**
   Social Studies:
   Strand: Individual Development and Identity
   3005.09 Identify and research the noble and brave qualities of an American hero

   Language Arts:
   1005.13 Uses writing as a tool across the curriculum
   1004.15 Uses organization to enhance understanding, uses a variety of organizational strategies (webbing, concept mapping, etc.)

Level: 5th-grade language arts/social studies   **Teacher's Name:**
Title: "Life Lines: Creating Timelines of a Life"
Time to Be Completed: Ten 60-minute sessions

One-Sentence Summary of the Assignment: What is the student to do? (Step 1) What will he have to show for it? (Step 4)

Students will work in small groups to research the life of a famous American, choose six key life events, write a paragraph about each event explaining why it is important, and construct a time-line of the events using the Read-Write-Think Timeline online.

Finished Product Evaluation: What are the criteria and method by which the student will be graded? (Step 4)

- Each group should cooperate to create a lifeline that:
  - Contains exactly six events, chosen by the group as the most important of the person's life
  - Describes each event fully and accurately
  - Uses correct grammar and spelling
  - Is based on three or more document sources that are reliable

Plan of Action: What activities will be used to reach the assignment outcomes? What new information will need to be presented? (Step 2)

Library Media Specialist

a. Go over the Handy 5 Assignment Planner
b. Help students locate resources, print and online
c. Teach students to use a citation worksheet
d. Model use of Read/Write/Think Timeline
e. Collaborate with classroom teacher in evaluating timelines using rubric

Classroom Teacher

a. Introduce project and assign famous persons
b. Show students a sample timeline
c. Assist students with taking notes
d. Facilitate group work and decision making
e. Collaborate with classroom teacher in evaluating timelines using rubric

Notes about Doing the Job: How is the unit developing; is the plan working? (Step 3)

A checklist of steps toward completion will be a tool for the students, as well as for the teacher/librarian, to use to determine each group's progress. It will include suggested completion dates for each task. As a group finishes a step and checks It off, completion can then be verified and initialed by the teacher.

Process Evaluation: How well did it go, what should be done differently next time? Documentation for student achievement, i.e., % of students reaching benchmark. (Step 5)

Incorporated into section 5 of the assignment planner would be questions soliciting feedback from the students about what they liked about the experience and what they thought could be improved, such as:

Student Assessment Measures: (Student product that assesses each step)
1. Assignment—Fill out sections one–four of the Assignment Planner
2. Plan of Action—Develop checklist
3. Doing the Job—Data chart
4. Product Evaluation—Rubric
5. Process Evaluation—Fill out section five of the Assignment Planner

Materials/Resources: Include only special requirements.

Computer access to databases for each group, preferably each student, books, encyclopedias, and other hard copy resources, student packets containing: Handy 5 Assignment Planner, checklist of tasks to completion, data gathering chart, citation worksheet, a sample timeline, and a copy of the rubric

CATEGORY	4	3	2	1
Number of Events	The timeline includes exactly 6 events.	The timeline includes only 5, or more than 6 events.	The timeline includes only 4 events.	The timeline includes less than 4 events.
Content/Facts	Events chosen are key events, described fully and accurately.	Some events chosen are not key events, OR are not described fully and accurately.	Most events chosen are not key events, OR are not described fully and accurately.	No events chosen are key events, OR are described fully and accurately.
Grammar and Spelling	Completed timeline has no more than 1 error in grammar or spelling.	Completed timeline has 2-3 errors in grammar or spelling.	Completed timeline has 4-5 errors in grammar or spelling.	Completed timeline has more than 5 errors in grammar or spelling.
Sources of Information	Documented use of 3 or more reliable sources of information.	Documented use of 2 reliable sources of information, OR 1 source used was not reliable.	Documented use of only 1 reliable source of information, OR 2 sources used were not reliable.	No sources documented were reliable sources.
Cooperative Group Work	Classroom time was used to work on the project. Conversations were not disruptive and focused on the work.	Classroom time was used to work on the project the majority of the time. Conversations were not disruptive and focused on the work.	Classroom time was used to work on the project the majority of the time, but conversations often were disruptive or did not focus on the work.	Student did not use classroom time to work on the project and/or was highly disruptive.

International Reading Association and National Council of Teachers of English. "Timeline." *Read/Write/Think*, 2002, at www.readwritethink.org/student_mat/student_material.asp?id=7

Collaborative Planning Outline   **Grade Six—Mathematics**

Standards Accomplished Addressed
Where does this assignment fit? What curriculum objectives will it fulfill?

1. Library Media Standards:
Standard 3: The student who is information literate uses information accurately and creatively.
Benchmark 4: Produces and communicates information and ideas in appropriate formats.

2. Collaborative Content Standards:
Geometry:
Standard 3: Geometry—The student uses geometric concepts and procedures in a variety of situations.
Benchmark 1: Geometric Figures and Their Properties—The student recognizes geometric figures and compares their properties in a variety of situations.

Level: 6th-grade mathematics   **Teacher's Name:**
Title: "A Medieval Math Adventure"
Time to Be Completed: Ten 45-minute sessions

One-Sentence Summary of the Assignment: What is the student to do? (Step 1) What will he have to show for it? (Step 4)

Students will demonstrate knowledge of angles and triangles while creating cardboard box castles and personal coat of arms

Finished Product Evaluation: What are the criteria and method by which the student will be graded? (Step 4)

- Use and citation of a minimum of three medieval resources
- Creation of preliminary sketches for castle and coat of arms
- Ability to work cooperatively when designing and creating castle
- Creativity in castle and coat of arms design
- Ability to relate angles and triangles to final products (must complete checklist/explanation sheet)
- Neatness in final products
- Each part of the project turned in by or before the due date
- Presentation of coat of arms to the class

Plan of Action: What activities will be used to reach the assignment outcomes? What new information will need to be presented? (Step 2)

Library Media Specialist	**Classroom Teacher**
a. Read books/section of books about the Middle Ages	a. Introduce project
b. Teach/assist students in locating a variety of print and non-print sources	b. Create/oversee cooperative groups
c. Provide feedback on sketches	c. Provide feedback on angle and triangle explanation presentations
d. Teach simple bibliography to cite references	d. Provide assistance with creation of castles
e. Review elements of an oral presentation	e. Allow class time for projects
f. Model good speaking skills	f. Provide checklist/explanation sheet and oral presentation rubric
g. Evaluate oral presentations	g. Evaluate oral and visual presentations
h. Display castles in the library	

Notes about Doing the Job: How is the unit developing; is the plan working? (Step 3)

Students need more practice locating bibliographical information. Students who changed ideas/designs without making a new sketch really struggled with their final product. Students need to master the types of angles and triangles before they begin group projects. Cutting the cardboard takes longer than expected. Need more practice with oral presentations and informal public speaking.

Process Evaluation: How well did it go, what should be done differently next time? Documentation for student achievement, i.e., % of students reaching benchmark. (Step 5)

Need more castle books that explain and show the basic structural parts of castles. Create handout for students that show and define many of the common designs for the coat of arms. Important to model a variety of ways to do an oral presentation. Consider inviting guest speakers to the classroom throughout the year so that students are exposed to a variety of public speaking styles. Next time do this unit in early fall so projects can be displayed for conferences. The coat of arms look nice mounted on 12 X 18 black construction paper.

Student Assessment Measures: (Student product that assesses each step)
1. Assignment—Students explain assignment to each other in small groups
2. Plan of Action—Initial completion of checklist and explanation sheet, initial discussion and attempts at creating sketches of coat of arms and castle
3. Doing the Job—Observation, worked cooperatively, completion of sketches for coat of arms (individual) and castle (group), creation of products
4. Product Evaluation—Coat of arms rubric, castle checklist and explanation sheet
5. Process Evaluation—Brainstorm most challenging, most fun, things that could be changed, what was learned?

Materials/Resources: Include only special requirements.

General resource materials about Middle Ages, including specific information about castles and coat of arms, checklist/explanation sheet, oral presentation rubric, cardboard/shoe boxes and craft materials such as glue, scissors, string, paints, and markers needed for creation of castles and coat of arms, Internet/computer lab

Checklist / Explanation Sheet for Medieval Math Unit

Define and draw each of the following:

ANGLES
   A. Right angle:

   B. Obtuse angle:

   C. Straight angle:

TRIANGLES
   D. Right triangle:

   E. Obtuse triangle:

   F. Acute triangle:

   G. Scalene triangle:

   H. Isosceles triangle:

   I. Equilateral triangle:

Please put a checkmark next to each angle or triangle used in your projects. Include a brief explanation of where the angle or triangle is located.

Object Type	√ if used	Where was it used?
Right angle		
Obtuse angle		
Straight angle		
Right triangle		
Obtuse triangle		
Acute triangle		
Scalene triangle		
Isosceles triangle		
Equilateral triangle		

List at least two things that you liked about your group experience:

List any part of your group experience that was not successful or was frustrating:

Collaborative Planning Outline   **Grade Six—Social Studies**

Standards Accomplished Addressed
Where does this assignment fit? What curriculum objectives will it fulfill?

1. **Library Media Standards:**
   Standard 5: The student who is an independent learner is information literate and appreciates literature and other creative expressions of information.
   Benchmark 2: Derives meaning from information presented creatively in a variety of formats.
   Benchmark 3: Develops creative products in a variety of formats.

   Standard 8: The student who contributes positively to the learning community and to society is information literate and practices ethical behavior in regard to information and information technology.
   Benchmark 2: Respects intellectual property rights.

2. **Collaborative Content Standards:**
   Geography:
   The student uses a working knowledge and understanding of the spatial organization of Earth's surface and relationships between peoples and places and physical and human environments in order to explain the interactions that occur in Kansas, the United States, and in our world.
   Benchmark 4: Human Systems: The student understands how economic, political, cultural, and social processes interact to shape patterns of human populations, interdependence, cooperation, and conflict.

   History:
   Standard: The student uses a working knowledge and understanding of significant individuals, groups, ideas, events, eras, and developments in the history of Kansas, the United States, and the world, utilizing essential analytical and research skills.
   Benchmark 4: The student engages in historical thinking skills.

Level: 6th-grade social studies   **Teacher's Name:**
Title: "Remember the Renaissance"
Time to Be Completed: Ten 45-minute sessions

One-Sentence Summary of the Assignment: What is the student to do? (Step 1) What will he have to show for it? (Step 4)

Students will design and create a brochure after researching the Renaissance, including the economy, social structure, political structure, religion, technology, and aesthetics.

Finished Product Evaluation: What are the criteria and method by which the student will be graded? (Step 4)

- Uses and cites at least three sources.
- Content is accurate–social structure, politics, religion, technology, and aesthetics are included.
- New vocabulary included.
- Writing conventions used.
- Finished product is well organized and attractive.
- Graphics and pictures are included and relate to the topic.

Plan of Action: What activities will be used to reach the assignment outcomes? What new information will need to be presented? (Step 2)

Library Media Specialist	**Classroom Teacher**
a. Help students formulate research questions	a. Introduce the unit and project
b. Guide students' expert group research including note taking and citing sources	b. Introduce the graphic organizer
	c. Divide student into expert research groups
c. Assist students with creation of brochure, planning and creation	d. Oversee expert groups' class presentations
d. Evaluate completed brochure	e. Evaluate completed brochure

Notes about Doing the Job: How is the unit developing; is the plan working? (Step 3)

Expert groups worked well together finding and sharing resources. Need to allow more time for expert groups' sharing. Students enjoyed creating brochure.

Process Evaluation: How well did it go; what should be done differently next time? Documentation for student achievement, i.e., % of students reaching benchmark. (Step 5)

Students were able to fill in the graphic organizer. Completed graphic organizer made designing the content of the brochure simpler.

Student Assessment Measures: (Student product that assesses each step)
1. Assignment—Quick write of directions.
2. Plan of Action—Timeline for expert group, research notes and presentation, brochure.
3. Doing the Job—Observation, check graphic organizer.
4. Product Evaluation—Rubric.
5. Process Evaluation—Class discussion of process, what did students enjoy, learn from projects, suggestions for changing for next year's class?

Materials/Resources: Include only special requirements.

Graphic organizer, brochure planning sheet, Renaissance resources including encyclopedia, nonfiction books, 6th-grade social studies text and websites

Collaborative Planning Outline   **Grade Seven—Science**

Standards Accomplished Addressed
Where does this assignment fit? What curriculum objectives will it fulfill?

1. **Library Media Standards:**
   Standard 1: The student who is information literate accesses information efficiently and effectively.

2. **Collaborative Content Standards:**
   Science:
   The learner will research and perform an experiment using scientific method to explore an agent of erosion.

Level: 7th-grade science   **Teacher's Name:**
Title: "Types of Erosion"
Time to Be Completed: Twenty 50-minute sessions

One-Sentence Summary of the Assignment: What is the student to do? (Step 1) What will he have to show for it? (Step 4)

Students will demonstrate how to research erosion through various resources, and present their findings to the rest of the class through an experiment, PowerPoint presentation, and paper.

Finished Product Evaluation: What are the criteria and method by which the student will be graded? (Step 4)

- All required materials available at the end of project.
- Grammar and spelling are correct on all written work.
- Uses scientific notation process to write experiment notes.
- Analysis and conclusion reasonable.
- PowerPoint presentation follows development checklist.

Plan of Action: What activities will be used to reach the assignment outcomes? What new information will need to be presented? (Step 2)

Library Media Specialist

a. Review location of reference section.
b. Show correct search engines.
c. Help students locate resources.
d. Help students do correct citations.
e. Teach creation of website bibliographies.
f. Evaluate research papers and bibliographies.

Classroom Teacher

a. Introduce unit and content.
b. Set guidelines for the variety of resources and Internet limits.
c. Teach note-taking procedure.
d. Help students set up experiment, collect and record data.
e. Help students with analysis and conclusion.
f. Evaluate research papers and bibliographies.

Notes about Doing the Job: How is the unit developing; is the plan working? (Step 3)

The unit went well and students worked diligently on their reports and PowerPoint presentations.

Process Evaluation: How well did it go, what should be done differently next time? Documentation for student achievement, i.e., % of students reaching benchmark. (Step 5)

Need to leave more time to research in the library. Students cited research correctly and had good bibliographies. Leave more time for experiment. All students finished their projects and experiments and completed the outcome.

Student Assessment Measures: (Student product that assesses each step)
1. Assignment—List criteria for the project and the materials required for completion, i.e., data chart, PowerPoint
2. Plan of Action—Timeline for project, hypothetical statement, parameters of experiment, storyboard for PowerPoint
3. Doing the Job—Teacher/LMS observation of various processes, research notes, bib. citations
4. Product Evaluation—Student's use of rubric for experiment and PowerPoint presentation; teacher evaluation for PowerPoint and experiment (science); LMS evaluation of bibliography page
5. Process Evaluation—Daily reflection notes kept in science journal

Materials/Resources: Include only special requirements.

General reference materials, materials for experiments. Sand, water, dirt, rocks, hair dryer, tubs, twigs, tree

Collaborative Planning Outline   **Grade Seven—Science-Technology**

Standards Accomplished Addressed
Where does this assignment fit? What curriculum objectives will it fulfill?

1. **Library Media Standards:**
   Standard 1: The student who is information literate accesses information efficiently and effectively.
   Benchmark 4: Identifies a variety of potential sources of information.

   Standard 2: The student who is information literate evaluates information critically and competently.
   Benchmark 1: Determines accuracy, relevance, and comprehensiveness.

2. **Collaborative Content Standards:**
   Life Science:
   Standard 3: The student will apply process skills to explore and understand structure and function in living systems, reproduction and heredity, regulation and behavior, populations and ecosystems.
   Benchmark 5: Observe the diversity of living things and relate their adaptations to their survival or extinction.

   Computer/Technology:
   Students use technology tools to enhance learning, increase productivity, and promote creativity.

Level: 7th-grade science-technology   **Teacher's Name:**
Title: "Flower Power"
Time to Be Completed: Eighteen 50-minute sessions

One-Sentence Summary of the Assignment: What is the student to do? (Step 1) What will he have to show for it? (Step 4)

Students will choose a flower from a prepared list; locate, evaluate, select, and cite resources based on a list of required information; design and create a flower brochure in a desktop publishing format

Finished Product Evaluation: What are the criteria and method by which the student will be graded? (Step 4)

- Rubric specifying type, number, and evaluation of sources, information use in note taking, and correctness of works cited page.
- List detailing information needed for inclusion on flower brochure.
- Rubric analyzing desktop publishing requirements, use of white space, images, conventions, and organization.

Plan of Action: What activities will be used to reach the assignment outcomes? What new information will need to be presented? (Step 2)

Library Media Specialist

a. Define task with students, look at rubrics, create individual folders to organize research from note sheets.
b. Demonstrate possible resources, discuss qualities of a good website, review Kan-Ed resources.
c. Demonstrate and practice MLA form for works cited.
d. Provide time for students to work.
e. Display completed brochures at Curriculum Fair.

Classroom Teacher

a. Discuss expectations, choose topics, discuss flower vocabulary.
b. Show example of complete brochure.
c. Demonstrate brochure layout and how to import images, discuss printing.
d. Provide time for organizing information for brochure and desktop publishing.

Notes about Doing the Job: How is the unit developing; is the plan working? (Step 3)

Most students were confused about perennial, biennial, and annual plants as well as whether to research the wild or domesticated variety of the flower. Some students frequently needed reminders to stay on timeline. They prefer looking for images for their flowers rather than researching and taking notes! A few students had problems locating information on their flower. Progress for each student was discussed in individual conferences.

Process Evaluation: How well did it go; what should be done differently next time? Documentation for student achievement, i.e., % of students reaching benchmark. (Step 5)

Ninety percent of the students satisfactorily completed the assignment. The other ten percent just did not locate enough information to satisfy all requirements of the rubric, specifically on the required list of topics from science content area. Next time, checking for required elements will be done more frequently during research, and searching for images for their brochures will be limited to one class period. The topics with limited information will be removed from the list of topics. Next time, include time for students to apply the rubric to their own work before viewing teacher-rated rubric.

Student Assessment Measures: (Student product that assesses each step)
1. Assignment—Thumbs up-thumbs down for general understanding, check individually during work time.
2. Plan of Action—On third day of research, students will conference individually to review resources. Students will defend the quality of selected websites.
3. Doing the Job—At least five completed Flower Power Research Notes, one for each resource used.
4. Product Evaluation—Rubric (computer, library) and checklist (science).
5. Process Evaluation—Group discussion about the quality of information sources and brochure.

Materials/Resources: Include only special requirements.

Photo-quality paper and color printer for brochure printing, Kan-Ed portal

Name_____

Assessment Form for 7th-Grade Flower Power Project
Library/Information

Standard: Student who is information literate:

1. accesses information efficiently and effectively; Benchmark 4—identifies a variety of potential sources of information; Indicator—independently uses information sources and the accompanying technology.

2. evaluates information critically and competently; Benchmark 1—determines accuracy, relevance, and comprehensiveness; Indicator—compares and contrasts multiple sources to verify accuracy of information.

Information Location Evaluation

5   Student locates quality, appropriate information about topic. At least five sources must be used. At least one source must be a book or encyclopedia, a magazine, and one must be a quality web page. Additionally, sources for images must be located.

4
3   Student completes most of above requirements.
2
1   Student includes minimal information.
0   Student did not do the project.

Information Use

5   Note-taking sheets are completed accurately. Notes are in student's own words or with quotes indicating direct quotation.
4
3   Student completes most of the above requirements.
2
1   Student includes minimal information. Notes are not complete. Spelling is not correct.
0   Student did not do the project.

Works Cited

5   The works cited page includes a title and all sources used in the project including images. All of the appropriate spacing, punctuation, and alphabetizing have been done according to the handout on the MLA form. The words on the page are spelled correctly; it has been processed.
4
3   The works cited page is missing some of the required elements. Some of the spacing, punctuation, spelling, and alphabetizing are correct.
2
1   Many of the required elements are missing. Spacing, punctuation, spelling, and alphabetizing are not correct.
0   Student did not do the project.

Flower Power Brochure Rubric
7th-grade computers

Standard: Students use technology tools to enhance learning, increase productivity, and promote creativity.

1. Brochure is in landscape view with three columns.
         1   2   3   4   5   6   7   8   9   10

2. Information is logically organized on the brochure.
         1   2   3   4   5   6   7   8   9   10

3. Information is appropriately centered and spaced on brochure.
         1   2   3   4   5   6   7   8   9   10

4. All capitalization, punctuation, spelling, and grammar are correct.
         1   2   3   4   5   6   7   8   9   10

5. Pictures are sharp and very clear.
         1   2   3   4   5   6   7   8   9   10

6. There are a variety of pictures in color and composition.
         1   2   3   4   5   6   7   8   9   10

7. There is very little white space.
         1   2   3   4   5   6   7   8   9   10

8. Headings are the appropriate font size.
         1   2   3   4   5   6   7   8   9   10

9. Font is appropriate for style and size for the body of the brochure.
         1   2   3   4   5   6   7   8   9   10

10. Student consistently extended effort and remained on task.
         1   2   3   4   5   6   7   8   9   10

Flower Power Plant Brochure   Name_____
7th grade Science

                                         Flower_____

3.5.1 The student will apply process skills to explore and understand structure and function in living systems, reproduction and heredity, regulation and behavior, populations and ecosystems, and diversity and adaptations of organisms.

Benchmark 5—observe the diversity of living things and relate their adaptations to their survival or extinction. Indicator—concludes that species of animals, plants, and microorganisms may look dissimilar on the outside but have similarities in internal structures, developmental characteristics, chemical processes, and genomes.

General information
  • How it reproduces
  • At least three different color pictures
  • Height of plant
  • Annual, biennial, or perennial
  • Scientific name
(Need all of the above)   14____

Flower description
  • Color(s)
  • Size of bloom
  • Foliage color
(Need all of the above)   6____

How to Plant
  • Time of year
  • How far apart
  • How deep
  • # per hole or if needs to be divided
  • Fertilizer or not
  • Sun/shade
  • Area of world (or zone)
  • Type of soil
  • Watering
  • When to transplant
  • When and how to divide
  • Weed control
  • Pruning
(Need at least 7 of the above)   14____

Uses
  • Hanging plants
  • Bouquets
  • Rock gardens
  • Cut flowers
  • Beds or borders
  • Other
(Need at least 2 of the above)   4____

Other information
  • Care over winter
  • Relatives (varieties)
  • State flower
  • Meaning of name
  • Other interesting facts
(Need at least 4 of the above)   8____

                    Total_____

                    Percentage_____

Research Notes Flower Power

Use one sheet for each resource.

Student's Name:_____Name of Flower:_____

Type of Resource:___Book___Internet___Periodical___CD-ROM___Image___Encyclopedia

Author: _____

Title of Book or Name of Periodical:_____

Periodical Article:_____

Date If a web page, use the date you accessed the site. All others use the copyright date of the source._____

Name of Publisher:_____Where Published:_____

Page Numbers:_____Web Address:_____

Notes: List the notes in the appropriate column

General In-formation	Description	How to Plant	Uses	Other Misc.

Collaborative Planning Outline   **Grade Eight—Reading/Communications**

Standards Accomplished Addressed
Where does this assignment fit? What curriculum objectives will it fulfill?

1. **Library Media Standards:**
   Standard 3: The student who is information literate uses information accurately and creatively.
   Benchmark 1: Organizes information for practical application.

   Standard 8: The student who contributes positively to the learning community and to society is information literate and practices ethical behavior in regard to information and information technology.
   Benchmark 2: Respects intellectual property rights.

2. **Collaborative Content Standards:**
   Reading:
   The student uses paraphrasing and organizational skills to summarize information (e.g., stated and implied main ideas, main events, important details) from appropriate-level narrative, expository, technical, and persuasive texts in logical order.

Level: 8th-grade reading/communications   **Teacher's Name:**
Title: "What Do You Want to Be When You Grow Up?"
Time to Be Completed: Fifteen 90-minute sessions

One-Sentence Summary of the Assignment: What is the student to do? (Step 1) What will he have to show for it? (Step 4)

The students of the eighth grade will investigate seven aspects of a career of interest and will create a PowerPoint presentation of at least 8 slides to go with a speech to last at least 4 minutes that will describe their research results.

Finished Product Evaluation: What are the criteria and method by which the student will be graded? (Step 4)

- Completeness of project (all seven aspects of the career were researched or if student could not locate that aspect of the career, they explain why; presentation at least 8 slides; speech lasted at least 4 minutes)
- Quality of speech and PowerPoint presentation, including whether or not the order of the presentation was logical and included the important details to describe the career
- Correct use of parenthetical citations in presentation and correct creation of works cited page
- Quality of notes taken (as this may not transfer into a quality PowerPoint, this aspect will be graded separately)
- Quality of reflection in the students' self-evaluations

Plan of Action: What activities will be used to reach the assignment outcomes? What new information will need to be presented? (Step 2)

Library Media Specialist	**Classroom Teacher**
a. Present a PowerPoint on locating the various resources needed.	a. Teach/review paraphrasing, taking notes, and documenting sources, using same library resources.
b. Present several options for finding career information on a handout.	b. Assign pairs based on similarity of subjects to begin locating materials.
c. Review how to search the OPAC for resources; review how to fill out an interlibrary loan request form.	c. Provide time and examples for practicing the various steps of the research process.
d. Help students locate information; fill out requests for Interlibrary Loans.	d. Show students how to create a works cited page.
e. Help students bookmark pages they find on the Internet and use "self-sticking" notes to mark pages in books, pamphlets, and encyclopedias.	e. Demonstrate creation of a PowerPoint presentation.
	f. Supervise students during the various processes.
	g. Assess all documents and re-teach to those students who are unable to complete project with at least 70% proficiency.

Notes about Doing the Job: How is the unit developing; is the plan working? (Step 3)

Students need more help with the various parts of the note-taking part of the project: Maybe show several different types of note-taking in hopes that individual students will find a personal type suited to them: Give more examples and practice of citing resources.

Process Evaluation: How well did it go, what should be done differently next time? Documentation for student achievement, i.e., % of students reaching benchmark. (Step 5)

The project went well. Students seemed to enjoy the project in spite of some of the difficulties with the technical parts of the project. We will be prepared with more examples and more practice time another time we do the unit.

Student Assessment Measures: (Student product that assesses each step)
1. Assignment—List the various criteria of the assignment
2. Plan of Action—Choose career and look for resources from the handout
3. Doing the Job—Choose best resources, take notes, create the PowerPoint, and write the speech
4. Product Evaluation—Check off each step of timeline, all documents created during the project, PowerPoint and speech
5. Process Evaluation—A reflection and self-evaluation of the research process

Materials/Resources: Include only special requirements.

Schedule use of technology (computer lab, computer projector, screen, Smart Board) and library space.

Collaborative Planning Outline   **Grade Eight—Social Studies**

Standards Accomplished Addressed
Where does this assignment fit? What curriculum objectives will it fulfill?

1. **Library Media Standards:**
   Standard 3: The student who is information literate uses information accurately and creatively.

2. **Collaborative Content Standards:**
   Social Studies:
   Demonstrates an understanding of patterns of change and continuity in the historical succession of related events.

Level: 8th-grade Civics   **Teacher's Name:**
Title: "Who Is in the Bill of Rights?"
Time to Be Completed: Fifteen-twenty 50-minute sessions

One-Sentence Summary of the Assignment: What is the student to do? (Step 1) What will he have to show for it? (Step 4)

Students will choose one "right" (Article) from the Bill of Rights, locate and record how the historical perspective has changed over time, and present to the class a documented pick-a-project about either a character who affected change, or an individual who was affected by change.

Finished Product Evaluation: What are the criteria and method by which the student will be graded? (Step 4)

- Used a variety of sources
- Logical connection between product and core material
- Presents core material in a new manner
- Reflects the change the character made or experiences
- Accompanied by documentation
- Completeness, neatness, and timelines of project

Plan of Action: What activities will be used to reach the assignment outcomes? What new information will need to be presented? (Step 2)

Library Media Specialist

a. Introduce project; present pick-a-project list
b. Demonstrate research steps and techniques
c. Assist with research
d. Provide supplies if requested
e. Videotape presentations

Classroom Teacher

a. Introduce Bill of Rights
b. Provide class research time, instruction
c. Work with students on characteristics of genres and projects
d. Collaborate in assessment

Notes about Doing the Job: How is the unit developing; is the plan working? (Step 3)

Some students have difficulty in choosing just one Article from the Bill of Rights.

Process Evaluation: How well did it go, what should be done differently next time? Documentation for student achievement, i.e., % of students reaching benchmark. (Step 5)

Student projects were well executed but I felt pressed time-wise in assisting students with locating resources.

Student Assessment Measures: (Student product that assesses each step)
1. Assignment—Written statement outlining assigned project
2. Plan of Action—Define a strategy for finding information
3. Doing the Job—Completed note cards and source cards
4. Product Evaluation—Project and documentation
5. Process Evaluation—Student self-evaluation from viewing videotape

Materials/Resources: Include only special requirements.

Reference materials, poster boards, markers, other art supplies, video camera, and videotapes

Collaborative Planning Outline   **Grade Nine–Foreign Language–Spanish**

Standards Accomplished Addressed
Where does this assignment fit? What curriculum objectives will it fulfill?

1. **Library Media Standards:**
   Standard 2: The student who is information literate evaluates information crucially and competently.
   Benchmark 4: Selects information appropriate to the problem or question at hand.

2. **Collaborative Content Standards:**
   Foreign Language–Spanish:
   Benchmark: 5.1.2 The student connects with the target culture through the use of technology, media, and authentic resources.

Level: High School Spanish I   **Teacher's Name:**
Title: "Introduction to the World of Spanish"
Time to Be Completed: Four 50-minute sessions

One-Sentence Summary of the Assignment: What is the student to do? (Step 1) What will he have to show for it? (Step 4)

Students will research a Spanish-speaking country using various websites including ones for that country and create a class book using the information.

Finished Product Evaluation: What are the criteria and method by which the student will be graded? (Step 4)

- Information from assigned country, cited sources for flag, maps, leader (president, king), 2 famous people, and a place of interest, weather conditions, and one item of choice.
- Cover with appropriate heading, table of contents.
- Overall appearance and accuracy of information.
- Effective use of time on task.

Plan of Action: What activities will be used to reach the assignment outcomes? What new information will need to be presented? (Step 2)

Library Media Specialist

a. Discuss research strategies with students.
b. Assist as needed in finding information.
c. Assist as needed in creating book.
d. Assess students' time on task.

Classroom Teacher

a. Check for students' knowledge of Spanish-speaking countries.
b. Discuss influence of the Spanish language and culture in the U.S. and chosen state.
c. Introduce the assignment.
d. Assess product and accuracy of information through the use of a checklist.

Notes about Doing the Job: How is the unit developing; is the plan working? (Step 3)

Check for adequate time allowances. Observe student time on task. Check for appropriate use of resources.

Process Evaluation: How well did it go, what should be done differently next time? Documentation for student achievement, i.e., % of students reaching benchmark. (Step 5)

Do students need more time/less time for research/project? How does the use of time for project relate to overall time needed for unit? Is the level of difficulty appropriate for the assignment and students? What percent of students made an 80% or better on the assignment? Does the rubric provide an accurate assessment of the project?

Student Assessment Measures: (Student product that assesses each step)
1. Assignment—Short written paragraph of what the assignment requires
2. Plan of Action—List of procedures the student plans to use to complete the project
3. Doing the Job—Observation of time on task, locating, accessing, and using information
4. Product Evaluation—Rubric evaluating the book
5. Process Evaluation—Student self-evaluation

Materials/Resources: Include only special requirements.

Internet access, art materials, printer, binding materials

Collaborative Planning Outline   **Grade Nine—Mathematics**

Standards Accomplished Addressed
Where does this assignment fit? What curriculum objectives will it fulfill?

1. **Library Media Standards:**
   Standard 3: The student who is information literate uses information accurately and creatively.

2. **Collaborative Content Standards:**
   Algebra:
   Student will multiply and divide integers.

Level: 9th-grade algebra   **Teacher's Name:**
Title: "Multiplying and Dividing Integers"
Time to Be Completed: One 70-minute session

One-Sentence Summary of the Assignment: What is the student to do? (Step 1) What will he have to show for it? (Step 4)

Students will apply rules to create and solve real-life problems involving multiplication and division of integers and present them on a poster board to the class.

Finished Product Evaluation: What are the criteria and method by which the student will be graded? (Step 4)

- Display and examples are clear, complete, and accurate.
- Mathematical language used appropriately and accurately.
- Display is neat, organized, and instructional.

Plan of Action: What activities will be used to reach the assignment outcomes? What new information will need to be presented? (Step 2)

Library Media Specialist

a. Show *Integer*, a video to provide an introduction to multiplication and division.
b. Gather resources (magazines, newspapers).
c. Assist the students with writing and editing their creative example.

Classroom Teacher

a. Explain assignment.
b. Assist during search activity.
c. Oversee writing and creation of examples.
d. Oversee work on displays.
e. Evaluate final product and presentation.

Notes about Doing the Job: How is the unit developing; is the plan working? (Step 3)

Students were able to use the checklist to help them complete the project successfully. They had no trouble finding examples in the magazines or newspaper. Combining math rules and world problems really helped students understand the math concept.

Process Evaluation: How well did it go, what should be done differently next time? Documentation for student achievement, i.e., % of students reaching benchmark. (Step 5)

Students developed a follow-up activity of creating examples and displaying them on poster boards. They were very pleased with their accomplishments.

Student Assessment Measures: (Student product that assesses each step)
1. Assignment—Write a list of the criteria for the assignment
2. Plan of Action—Find examples from newspapers and magazines
3. Doing the Job—Observation of writing and editing of their examples
4. Product Evaluation—Use rubric for oral presentation and visual displays shared with classmates
5. Process Evaluation—Class discussion reflecting on process

Materials/Resources: Include only special requirements.

Newspapers and magazines, poster board, art supplies, *Integer* video

Collaborative Planning Outline   **Grade Ten—Social Studies**

Standards Accomplished Addressed
Where does this assignment fit? What curriculum objectives will it fulfill?

1. **Library Media Standards:**
   Reading and Writing:
   Standard 5.2.1 Determine relevance of information for specific needs.
   Standard 5.2.2 Organize and synthesize information about a topic from a variety of sources.

2. **Collaborative Content Standards:**
   World History:
   1.1.4 Describe the impact of the major people and events of each era.
   1.2.1 Students use chronology to examine historical relationships.

Level: 10th–grade World Cultures & Geography   **Teacher's Name:**
Title: "Crossroads of History Quest"
Time to Be Completed: Four 90-minute sessions; two will be in the library

One-Sentence Summary of the Assignment: What is the student to do? (Step 1) What will he have to show for it? (Step 4)

Students in groups will select and research a person or event and their impact from the Renaissance, Reformation, or Exploration periods and will create a board game to present the information to the class that includes a map, a timeline, images, and descriptive paragraphs.

Finished Product Evaluation: What are the criteria and method by which the student will be graded? (Step 4)

Assessment will be based on the following factors:
- Critical thinking
- Knowledge and use of history
- Quality of final product
- Group participation

Plan of Action: What activities will be used to reach the assignment outcomes? What new information will need to be presented? (Step 2)

Library Media Specialist

a. Assist with topic selection using www.timelineindex.com.
b. Present graphic organizer.
c. Instruct and guide students with selecting, locating, and citing multiple sources.
d. Instruct and assist students with note-taking.

Classroom Teacher

a. Introduce project and rubric.
b. Monitor progress.
c. Facilitate cooperative group discussions and encourage critical thinking.
d. Lead group presentations to class.

Notes about Doing the Job: How is the unit developing, is the plan working? (Step 3)

Have teacher/librarian approve inquiry topic and questions before students begin research. Need to remind students to be aware of the reliability of sources they are choosing, since instruction on source evaluation is not a component of this unit. Require students to check in with the status of their research notes before beginning final product.

Process Evaluation: How well did it go; what should be done differently next time? Documentation for student achievement, i.e., % of students reaching benchmark. (Step 5)

May need a planning tool that is separate from the research phase for students to propose the final product. Some students may get bogged down in preparing the game after they finish the research or rush ahead before research is completed. May need additional class time for production. Librarian might want to include a citation worksheet on the reverse side of the graphic organizer.

Student Assessment Measures: (Student product that assesses each step)
1. Assignment—Think-Pair-Share
2. Plan of Action—Research questions on graphic organizer
3. Doing the Job—Information reported on graphic organizer
4. Product Evaluation—Rubric
5. Process Evaluation—Self-evaluation questionnaire

Materials/Resources: Include only special requirements.

Bookmark www.timelineindex.com website on computers, make copies of rubric, graphic organizer, and self-evaluation forms, prepare book cart or pathfinder if teacher requests, arts materials for final product

Rubric for Crossroads of History Project

	4	3	2	1
Critical Thinking Standards: History 1.1.4 English 5.2.1	The premise of the game requires a thorough and complex understanding of subject of investigation by inventing a new or different version of history and accurately identifying the people or events most impacted by the resulting change. (How would … be different if…)	The premise of the game requires a thorough understanding by inventing a new or different version of history that involves key defining moments involving the subject of investigation. (What if … had never happened)	The premise of the game accurately addresses details about the subject of investigation. (Who, What, When Where, Why, and How)	Not enough work produced or completed correctly to assess.
Knowledge and Use of History Standards: History 2.1.2 English 5.3.2	Demonstrates a clear, accurate understanding of subject of investigation and its impacts on world history. Employs personal knowledge and correctly cites information from various sources that are relevant, accurate, and consistent.	Demonstrates clear understanding of subject of investigation and some consideration of consequences. Employs personal knowledge and correctly cites information from at least two sources that are factual.	Demonstrates a general understanding of the subject of investigation. Limited examination of evidence using the general idea or main points from personal knowledge and at least one source of information.	Not enough work produced or completed correctly to assess.
Quality of Final Product Standards: History 1.2.1 English 5.3.3	Game is related to theme, is presented imaginatively, and effectively flows logically from beginning to end. Physical appearance of project shows sophistication and attention to detail. Includes a map, a timeline, images, and descriptive paragraphs.	Game is related to the theme, is interesting, and adequately flows from beginning to end. Good physical appearance of project. Minor flaws in attention to detail. Includes descriptive paragraphs and either a map, a timeline, or images.	Game shows vague references to the theme. Overall project lacks clarity or is missing vital elements. Serious errors in attention to detail.	Not enough work produced or completed correctly to assess.
Group Participation Standards: History 1.2.1 English 5.3.3	Almost all students enthusiastically participate. Responsibility for task is shared.	At least 3/4 students actively participate. Discussion mostly centers on the task.	Only one or two persons actively participate. Conversation not entirely centered on topic. Some students are disinterested or distracted.	Exclusive reliance on one spokesperson. Little interaction.

Name: _____

Class: _____

My Topic: _____

_____

Directions:
Think about your effort on this project and what you learned. Fill out the chart considering what you did well, and how you might improve next time.

	What I did well:	What I could do better:
How well did you understand what to do? Was the assignment clear? If not, what did you do?		
What kinds of resources did you use (books, websites, etc)? Were they helpful? What other resources could you have found and used?		
Was it easy to find the answers to your questions? Did you have trouble finding or understanding the information?		
Were you able to identify the important parts and pull out just the information you needed?		
Did you completely answer the questions? Did you organize and present the information in a way that makes sense to others?		
Did you use your time well? What was your contribution to the group? What personal skills did you use or do you need to work on?		

Data Organizer

Name: _____

Class: _____

My Topic: _____

_____

Directions:
1. Write your selected person or event from the Renaissance, Reformation, or Exploration periods in the center circle.
2. Fill in who, what, where, when, why, and how questions as you find the information in different sources.
3. Select one additional "What if..." question to research in the top box. This question will become the premise of your board game.

How would _____
be different if _____?

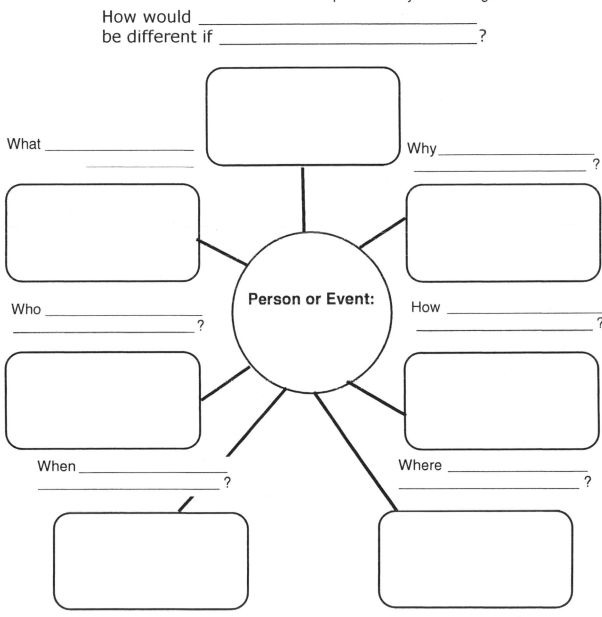

Collaborative Planning Outline   **Grade Ten—Language Arts**

Standards Accomplished Addressed
Where does this assignment fit? What curriculum objectives will it fulfill?

1. **Library Media Standard: (Embedded in Language Arts Standards)**
   Reading Standard III (A): Students will demonstrate understanding of information texts.

   Reading Standard III (B): Students conduct research using a variety of grade-appropriate sources.

2. **Collaborative Content Standards:**
   Reading:
   Standard II (A): Students demonstrate an understanding of literary text.

Level: 10th-grade World Literature   **Teacher's Name:**
Title: "What's Culture Got to Do With It?"
Time to Be Completed: Ten 80-minute sessions

One-Sentence Summary of the Assignment: What is the student to do? (Step 1) What will he have to show for it? (Step 4)

Students will produce an annotated bibliography from research about a country from their world literature text, and they present what they discovered from research about their selected country in an oral presentation.

Finished Product Evaluation: What are the criteria and method by which the student will be graded? (Step 4)

- Annotated bibliographies must be in MLA format and include five sources, 12-point plain font, double space between entries.
- Finished product for research will include source evaluations. Colored construction paper will be used to mat each illustration.
- Presentations will be 3-8 minutes in length with a minimum of two visual aids, one of which must be a map of their country.
- Content of presentations must include findings from research that was stimulated by cultural elements present in their literature selection. They must reference their selection in the presentation and conclude with their understanding of how culture influences literature.
- Students will conduct research and present the research according to the rubric provided to them in class.

Plan of Action: What activities will be used to reach the assignment outcomes? What new information will need to be presented? (Step 2)

Library Media Specialist	Classroom Teacher
a. Annotated bibliographic instruction	a. Story selection
b. Summarizing practice	b. Cultural influence
c. Database search	c. Essential questioning
d. Source evaluations	d. Research expectations
e. Note-taking skills	e. Presentation skills
f. Research preparation	f. Outline explanation

Notes about Doing the Job: How is the unit developing; is the plan working? (Step 3)

Students are progressing well. Some are having trouble finding the exact information they need for their chosen country. Gave permission to change questions to match materials. I have given them goals for the number of sources they should have after each day of research to keep them on track. Only one or two seem to be having difficulty focusing on the task and finding information.

Process Evaluation: How well did it go; what should be done differently next time? Documentation for student achievement, i.e., % of students reaching benchmark. (Step 5)

Overall the lesson went very well. My students had never seen an annotated bibliography, so need to model this next time, have more in-class practice.

On the first day there were many questions; by the last they understood the idea of hit-and-miss search terms, were able to navigate to the information they needed. Check that information is available earlier in the process. Collect source evaluation sheets at the end of each period to monitor student progress.

Student Assessment Measures: (Student product that assesses each step)
1. Assignment—Paragraph of student's understanding of the assignment.
2. Plan of Action—In-class summary and bibliography practice, research prep sheet.
3. Doing the Job—Note cards, bibliography cards, source evaluations, verbal progress check.
4. Product Evaluation—Presentation (speaking, listening rubric) and annotated bibliography teacher research rubric.
5. Process Evaluation—Student research rubric.

Materials/Resources: Include only special requirements.

Library materials (books and computers), LCD projector for presentations

Collaborative Planning Outline   **Grade Eleven—Science**

Standards Accomplished Addressed
Where does this assignment fit? What curriculum objectives will it fulfill?

1. **Library Media Standards:**
   Standard 2: The student who is information literate evaluates information critically and competently.
   Benchmark 1: Determines accuracy, relevance, and comprehensiveness.
   Benchmark 4: Selects information appropriate to the problem or question at hand.

2. **Collaborative Content Standards:**
   Science:
   Standard 2A: The student will develop an understanding of the structure of atoms, compounds, chemical reactions, and the interactions of energy and matter.
   Benchmark 1.1: The student will understand the structure of an atom.

Level: 11th-grade Chemistry   **Teacher's Name:**
Title: "You're in Your Element"
Time to Be Completed: Fifteen 50-minute sessions

One-Sentence Summary of the Assignment: What is the student to do? (Step 1) What will he have to show for it? (Step 4)

The student will research an element to determine its history, group, properties, occurrence, and uses resulting in a research paper, a Christmas ornament, and an oral presentation.

Finished Product Evaluation: What are the criteria and method by which the student will be graded? (Step 4)

- Research paper covering history, group, properties, occurrence, uses, and one interesting fact about the assignment element
- Cover page showing picture of common use of the element, element name, and atomic number—in vertical format on the page (to be hung on wall demonstrating the Periodic Table of Elements)
- Element ornament—3D replica of any substance that contains the element or simulation of the element (size: minimum 3 cubic cm; maximum 12 cubic cm)
- Oral presentation using attention-getting introduction, one statement for each topic paragraph of written report, use of visual aid (cover sheet), use of element ornament and summary closing, not to exceed 10 minutes

Plan of Action: What activities will be used to reach the assignment outcomes? What new information will need to be presented? (Step 2)

Library Media Specialist

a. Introduce Boolean search strategy
b. Review on-line databases and in-
    dices
c. Assist in developing a plan of ac-
    tion
d. Monitor research in LMC

Classroom Teacher

a. Present content information,
    assign elements
b. Monitor progress through deadlines
c. Evaluate oral presentation, orna-
    ment, and paper

Notes about Doing the Job: How is the unit developing; is the plan working? (Step 3)

Students appear at ease with the model and make good use of LMC time. Assignment is well structured, leaving little to chance or interpretation. Time period is a little short for all components, but the students are hustling.

Process Evaluation: How well did it go; what should be done differently next time? Documentation for student achievement, i.e., % of students reaching benchmark. (Step 5)

Boolean search strategy and online databases are almost too much for one assignment. Next time present Boolean search strategy in an earlier assignment.

Student Assessment Measures: (Student product that assesses each step)
1. Assignment—Reflective paragraph defining time schedule and parameters.
2. Plan of Action—Chart of search terms, ranking of sources.
3. Doing the Job—Timeline for components of the assignment to be due.
4. Product Evaluation—Paper, cover page, ornament, oral presentation.
5. Process Evaluation—Teacher evaluation of products using criteria listed above; student. evaluation of product and process (see following page).

Materials/Resources: Include only special requirements.

OPAC material records, periodical abstracts from Facts on File, NewsBank Reference Service, ProQuest GPO Research II, Reader's Guide, and General Science Index

Evaluate the Product

1. Did the oral and written reports have an attention-getting introduction?

2. Did the oral and written reports cover each of the following?
   * history of the element
   * chemical and physical properties
   * how it is obtained
   * how it is used today
   * advantages and disadvantages of its use

3. Did the oral and written reports have a summary closing?

4. Was the visual aid clear and concise?

5. Was the visual aid well produced?

6. Did the visual aid include the following?
   * element name
   * atomic mass
   * symbol
   * picture of how it is used

7. Was the element tree ornament unique and original?

8. Did the ornament appear to be well thought out and well constructed?

9. Was the ornament at least 3 cm cubed and no larger than 12 cm cubed?

Evaluate the Process

1. Did writing a description of the assignment help you understand better what you needed to do?

2. Did developing a research strategy prior to beginning the research help you organize the search, and save you time and/or frustration?

3. Did having specific dates for each step of the process help you keep on task?

4. In your own words, evaluate this assignment and the problem-solving process that was used.

Collaborative Planning Outline   **Grade Eleven—Social Studies**

Standards Accomplished Addressed
Where does this assignment fit? What curriculum objectives will it fulfill?

1. **Library Media Standards:**
   Standard 1: The student who is information literate accesses information efficiently and effectively.
   Benchmark 4: Identifies a variety of potential sources of information.

   Standard 5: The student who is an independent learner is information literate and appreciates literature and other creative expressions of information.
   Benchmark 3: Develops creative products in a variety of formats.

2. **Collaborative Content Standards:**
   History:
   Standard 4: The student uses a working knowledge and understanding of significant individuals, groups, ideas, events, eras, and developments in the history of Kansas, the United States, and the world, utilizing essential analytical and research skills.
   Benchmark 3: The student uses a working knowledge and understanding of individuals, groups, ideas, developments, and turning points in the Civil Rights era.

Level: 11th-grade history   **Teacher's Name:**
Title: "The Civil Rights Era and Kansas"
Time to Be Completed: Six 50-minute session in the classroom, four in the library

One-Sentence Summary of the Assignment: What is the student to do? (Step 1) What will he have to show for it? (Step 4)

Students will learn the difference between primary and secondary sources, researching for each, learning Microsoft Publisher, and creating written pieces based on their understanding of the sources

Finished Product Evaluation: What are the criteria and method by which the student will be graded? (Step 4)

- Demonstrates an understanding of primary and secondary sources.
- Demonstrates clear purpose and convention in the written portions.
- Participates in group activities.
- Shows original thought and connections to the material.
- Uses the rubrics to follow the outline.

Plan of Action: What activities will be used to reach the assignment outcomes? What new information will need to be presented? (Step 2)

Library Media Specialist	**Classroom Teacher**
a. Check for prior knowledge.	a. Check for prior knowledge.
b. Introduce primary/secondary sources.	b. Introduce and teach Civil Rights Era.
c. Demonstrate research process in library and online searching for these sources.	c. Introduce and teach Brown vs. Topeka BOE.
d. Introduce Microsoft Publisher.	d. Introduce assignments.
e. Discuss elements of a newsletter and newsletter.	e. Grade assignments.

Notes about Doing the Job: How is the unit developing; is the plan working? (Step 3)

The elements that needed the most oversight were understanding of the total assignment, time management, and use of the Publisher software.

Process Evaluation: How well did it go, what should be done differently next time? Documentation for student achievement, i.e., % of students reaching benchmark. (Step 5)

Students did well. The final products met our expectations. For next year develop a checklist of individual activities with a timeline to help with time management.

Student Assessment Measures: (Student product that assesses each step)
1. Assignment—Class discussion after receiving unit guidelines
2. Plan of Action—Notes on the value of primary/secondary sources presented by the LMS
3. Doing the Job—Teacher checks on use of primary/secondary sources, progress on newsletter
4. Product Evaluation—Rubrics for primary/secondary sources and newsletter
5. Process Evaluation—Brainstorm with class and collaborating teacher

Materials/Resources: Include only special requirements.

Bibliography of primary/secondary sources

Index

About the Authors

While the second edition contains much of the original work done by the Kansas Association of School Librarians Research Committee, several members of that group have updated that first edition.

Shelia K. Blume is the school librarian at F.L. Schlagle High School in Unified School District 500, Kansas City, Kansas. **Carol Fox** is a retired library media specialist and adjunct faculty member at Emporia State University School of Library and Information Management. **Jacqueline McMahon Lakin** is an information management consultant for the Kansas State Department of Education in Topeka. **Betsy Losey** is a retired elementary library media specialist who serves as chairman of the KASL Handy 5 Marketing Committee and is the editor for this edition. **Janis K. Stover** is the school librarian at Highland Park Central Elementary School in Unified School District 501, Topeka, Kansas.